PERSONALLY SPEAKING

Celebrating our Catholic Values and Ideals

Msgr. Jim Lisante

D0107393

Resurrection Press
An Imprint of
CATHOLIC BOOK PUBLISHING CO.
Totowa • New Jersey

To my best friend, Father Joe Lukaszewski
"the richest man in town."
1952 - 2000

Grateful acknowledgement is made to *The Long Island Catholic* to reproduce essays contained in these pages.

First published in September 2000 by
Catholic Book Publishing/Resurrection Press
77 West End Road
Totowa, NJ 07512

ISBN 1-878718-51-7
Library of Congress Catalog Card Number: 98-68011

Cover design by John Murello
Cover photo by Richard Muller, Franklin Square Photographers

Printed in Canada

Contents

Part I
HOLY LIVES

Part II
LIFE ISSUES

Part III
CELEBRITIES AND HEROES

Part IV
LOVING RELATIONSHIPS

Part V
21st CENTURY LIVING

Acknowledgements

AS the Pastor of St. Thomas the Apostle Parish in West Hempstead, New York, I spend a lot of time saying thank you. I love being the Pastor of this dynamic, faith-filled and deeply kind community of believers. They support me in ways that truly sustain me, and they keep me loving my priesthood. During the long and challenging time when I brought my best friend Joe Lukaszewski into St. Thomas to live out his remaining days of earthly life, they truly upheld me.

I also want to thank my incredibly loving personal family. They sensitize me to life like no one else. So thanks Mom and Dad, Patti and Bob, Joan and Jim, Matthew, Jonathan, Anthony, Marisa and Julia for surrounding me with your love and goodness.

My writing is encouraged and promoted by friends like Monsignor Frank Maniscalco and Ms. Liz O'Connor. This book is here because of Emilie Mackney and Nancy de Flon. My television ministry grows because of the Catholic Communications Campaign, the good people at Odyssey Cable Network, my producers Ellen McCloskey and Ken Stockard, and the National Conference of Catholic Bishops. Thank you all.

Finally, I am only able to do what I do because of the love and tenderness of my friends. So special gratitude must be expressed to: Father Brian Barr, Father Andrzej Zglejszewski, Father Paul Bie, Father Ken Marks, Father Andrew Vaccari, Father Bob Smith, Father Tom Brosnan, Msgr. Jim MacNamara, Father Ken Winkler, Msgr. Frank Caldwell, Father Ken Zach, Father Jack Maloney, Steve Gade, Steve Getty, John and Kathy Carlsen, Maria Milone, Patricia Neal, John and Maureen Raber, Val and Pat Caulfield, Corrine Lok, Susan Lawlor, Don and Joan Rudolph, Randy and Tom Slade, John and Phyllis Provost, Elaine and Tom Sedita, Richard and Mary Muller, Chris Robinson, Joanna and Jim Harrington, Toni Polumbo, Joe and Linda Mondello, David Benedict, Barbara and Nathaniel Schwartz, Carl Coppertino, John and Lois Donnelly, my personal assistants Elaine Harmon, Carol Burak and Peggy O'Donoghue, Jonathan Wood, Al D'Amato, Terri and Bill Rockensies, Meg DeGia, Phil and Carmen Quartararo, Matthew Kelly, Greg and Keith Muller, and the whole Eddie Smith family.

Thanks to Bishops John McGann and James McHugh, my bosses! Thanks to my friends in the Columbian Lawyers Association, Morality in Media and Priests for Life. And thanks to the Lord for His gift of life and love. Truly, all is His Grace!

Msgr. Jim Lisante and Cardinal William Keeler on the set of Msgr. Jim's Odyssey Network program "Personally Speaking."

Foreword

MONSIGNOR James Lisante hosts a television and radio program sponsored by the United States Catholic Conference called "Personally Speaking." It was as a guest on this program that I first became aware of Monsignor Jim's ability to reach an audience with his gentle but still penetrating manner. I was happy to discover that he is also a columnist in the Catholic press and that his columns have formed the basis of two previous volumes. I am glad to help present this third one.

On "Personally Speaking," Monsignor Lisante introduces viewers to Catholics who carry on the Church's pastoral service, including my brother Bishops. Among his guests are people who, through living their faith everyday, have a story that should be shared, as well as people of other faiths whose stories it is worthwhile for all to know.

In these brief essays, Monsignor Jim shows the same enthusiasm to share stories of faith which will inspire others. Many essays demonstrate his concern for young people and the challenges they face in growing up as believers in today's culture. Too often, this culture pays only lip service to belief in God and the values that flow from it. At its worst, it holds these things up to ridicule. As someone who knows contemporary culture and appreciates what's good in it, Monsignor Jim deals with these issues most persuasively.

As a priest, Monsignor Jim has devoted much of his ministry to pro-life issues, for which he is a much sought after spokesman around our nation. His commitment to defending the fundamental value of life from conception to natural death as well as his skill in rebutting these who embrace what Pope John Paul II has called the "culture of death," are apparent in these essays. At the same time, he reveals the Church's compassion for those who face difficult decisions or experience the pain of making the wrong ones.

A brief foreword cannot cover all the items of interest found here, and so I urge the prospective reader to open up *Personally Speaking* anywhere and start reading. You will not quickly put it down.

Cardinal William H. Keeler

Maxwell Caulfield, stage and film star. Read his extraordinary journey of faith on page 71.

Introduction

TO suggest in the preface of a Catholic priest's new book that the reader should immediately deface its contents by taking a "Hi-liter" pen to those passages that strike closest to home, is possibly sacreligious. For that I am sorry, but what else should you expect when you invite a Protestant Hollywood-based actor to introduce a collection of spiritual readings and thought provoking essays?

In an engaging conversational style, Monsignor Lisante acknowledges that Jim, the man, stubs his toe, feels tired and gets turned around almost as much as the rest of us. But since his vocation calls for, indeed mandates, that he stop to help a beleaguered stranger and take time to truly appreciate his surroundings, he is far better qualified than most to tend the travelers aid stand on the road to enlightenment. And even as we weary souls heap our sorrows and confusions (plus confessions, of course) upon him, Jim Lisante recognizes that he is in a position of special privilege . . . for he never lacks for friends, is constantly developing his levels of awareness and tolerance and at the end of the day truly knows where is is headed!

Which brings me back to my initial suggestion: that you do indeed take up that fluorescent pen and not only highlight the home truths and pearls of wisdom contained herein, but say out loud those self same words in order that they may stick— rather in the manner by which this humble thespian endeavors, ever so meekly, to learn his lines. So read, enjoy and consider. I know you will.

Maxwell Caulfield

Part I
Holy Lives

WWJD

AROUND the country, I'm often given the chance to speak to teenagers and young adults. It's not unusual to find a growing number of young people wearing bracelets or buttons which read "WWJD." And that question — What would Jesus do? — gives us a sure and confident road map for our own lives. Let's look at some of the specifics of how Jesus did live His life.

1. Unlike the simple-minded hero of "The Green Mile" Jesus was smart and used his intelligence well. He wasn't beyond a good debate and liked to intellectually challenge people. If we'd be like Him, we should celebrate our minds and use them for the good.

2. Clearly, Jesus avoided cursing, lying or swearing, but he wasn't a wimp either. He stated His case strongly and without equivocation. He also got angry and expressed it. We too often, I think, see anger as a totally bad thing. It's not always bad, especially when expressed in the name of justice. So that, for example, there's no sugar-coating the reality that Jesus was awfully upset at the merchants and sellers in the temple. And when he chased them out and condemned their mercenary business practices, that was justifiable and righteous anger. When you or I witness injustice, we too have a right to get upset and to express it. Jesus did that, too.

3. We know that Jesus would challenge people. He did it constantly in His public ministry. And He did it, time and time again, to those He loved the most, people like St. Peter. He did it to the woman he met at the well. He did it to the stone-throwers He met in the company of the adulterous woman. But, and this is important, He never purposely hurt anyone. His wisdom and insight, His hold on the truth did not give Him the license to cut people down, to make them feel stupid, or to calumniate them. Too often, I suspect, we think that because our point of view is sustainably right, we have the

right to belittle or reduce people who don't get it. And we don't. Not by Jesus' example, anyway. He would challenge, but always with respect for the other person. Rightness, He knew, doesn't entitle us to cruelty. So, for example, He does confront the sin of the woman caught in adultery. But He does it with gentleness, compassion and a clear choice for mercy.

4. In a consumer-driven world, we might well ask, "Did Jesus live for things?" And clearly the answer is, "No way!" This is an adult man who never owned a home, never had a savings account, never knew about having a wardrobe, never met a computer, and probably sang a bit, but never owned a compact disc. And, it seems, one who never suffered for the lack of earthly possessions. His life is a clear and unmistakable lesson which tells us that things alone will never make us complete. It's truth and love and service to others that matter. They're the things we bring with us to the other side of life.

5. It's become very trendy for people today to say of themselves, "Well, I'm not really a religious person, but I am deeply spiritual." They put a chasm between organized religion and its practice and what they think of as the deepening of their spiritual selves. That's something Jesus never did. He clearly and consistently practiced His Judaism. He attended temple and studied His faith. From His early years until the end of His earthly life, He took seriously the practices of His religion. At the same time, He also deepened His spiritual life through fasting and time at prayer. In other words, Jesus didn't separate religious practice from spiritual development. He observed them as two sides of the same coin.

6. Equivocation is really big in contemporary America. We can justify almost anything. We've become the people who can't or won't call anything really wrong. Some people call it moral relativism. They say nothing's clearly black or white, right or wrong, that nuance and grayness make things which might be wrong for you, right for another. That's clearly not

what Jesus would say or do. He taught directly and He called right what is right and named wrong as well. He didn't fudge it. He didn't equivocate. And, importantly, that clarity was always mixed with mercy and understanding. He understood the human sinful condition. He named it as such, but He also loved and forgave people in their human weakness. That, I suspect, is the route to human wholeness, not denying who we are or what we do, but accepting our human foibles, trying to heal our faults and getting spiritually and psychologically well.

7. Jesus went the distance. One of the complaints I most often hear about life in young America today is a lack of loyalty and consistency. Your best friends today may well be strangers tomorrow. The friend you bare your soul to this week may be sharing those secrets with others next week. And the cumulative effect of all this is a real lack of trust in others. That was never the way with Jesus. If He entered your life, He was there to stay. He taught us by His fidelity what true friendship ought to be, even when His friends did Him wrong. He gives up on no one.

Question for Reflection

● It's one thing to know what Jesus would do and another thing to live that way. Which of these seven points struck you as a way to begin?

To Die For

BACK in high school I read one terrific book by New York Post columnist Ray Kerrison. It was called *Bishop Walsh of Maryknoll* and told the story of a courageous missionary priest assigned to China. Bishop Walsh was born and raised in America but spent most of his adult life serving the people of China. He helped them physically, socially and spiritually. It was his misfortune and his opportunity to be stationed in China during the takeover of that country by Communist forces. The Marxist government systematically attempted to eradicate any non-Chinese influence, deporting most foreign missionaries. It didn't matter to the government that most of those like Bishop Walsh were only there to serve the needs of the poor. They were almost completely eliminated from the Chinese nation. Bishop Walsh refused to leave. He loved his people and felt his place was properly with them. For his faithfulness, this good and gentle soul endured the mockery of a trial, facing trumped-up charges of being a foreign spy. Upon conviction, Bishop Walsh was placed in prison. There he suffered humiliation and deprivation. His life often hung in the balance. To be released all he needed to do was confess that he was a spy or repudiate his faith. But for James Edward Walsh, neither of those choices was ever a possibility. To Bishop Walsh, some things are worth your life, like honor and faithfulness. From the late 1940s until the early 1970s Bishop Walsh languished in a wretched prison. Finally, in a trade worked out by the American government, the Communists shipped him home to the United States. Uncompromised, faithful to the end, Bishop Walsh returned to Maryknoll headquarters and lived out his life with the knowledge that he had fought the good fight and had never forsaken his values and his principles. Re-reading Kerrison's wonderful book makes me wonder about the choice made by Bishop Walsh. And it left me thinking that for most of us, his decision to put honor above all would make us fairly uncomfortable. I'm afraid we're living in a time where there's little which we value so deeply that we'd be willing to die for our choices.

But maybe I'm wrong. Maybe there is still a lot of nobility out there. Maybe we do value some ideals enough to "lay down our lives for our brothers and sisters," in what Jesus calls the ultimate sign of genuine love. Two examples come to mind. My friend, Joe, is a guy in his early 20s. He found out that his brother Terry needed a kidney transplant. Without it, Terry would not survive. Now Joe is no hero, but he loves his brother. Not that they, like any family, don't have their differences; but when push comes to shove, they're there for each other. The surgery wasn't without risk. In fact, with kidney disease a family tradition, it's surely possible that one day Joe may someday face a similar dilemma. And when and if his time of risk surfaces, Joe will be facing the prospect of trying to survive with only one kidney. I spoke to Joe shortly before he gave up a kidney for his brother. He was simple and classic. "What choice do I really have?" he pondered. "My brother's in trouble, and he needs my help. Talk about love is just so many words if you're not willing to go the distance." Joe did, in fact, give his kidney. There were side effects. There is risk. But Terry is alive and well, and that's because he has a brother who cares and put the force of doing behind his concern.

Or consider Shannon Smith. Just 20 years old, he was sliding down a natural stream with teammates on a recent outing. His football coach entrusted his six-year-old son, Cody, to Shannon's care as they happily barreled down the water slide.

But when they got to the pool below, something was wrong. A whirlpool had been created which sucked Shannon and Cody into its center. As bystanders attempted a rescue, Shannon kept pushing the boy to the surface. He drowned so that Cody could live.

Shannon could easily have excused himself for leaving the child in order to save himself. But this young man had a sense of honor and responsibility; and saving a six-year-old was, he felt, worth his life. Bishop Walsh, my friend Joe, and Shannon Smith all have something in common. They believed that we're here not simply to get but to give. They thought that some values are worth your life. They were willing to place their lives on the line because higher values were at stake. We are not, as some say, a society without generous values. There are, in fact, people who live and love and give and protect all around us. They should be celebrated.

Questions for Reflection

- Recall a time when you played the Good Samaritan to someone in need. How did you feel doing it? How did you feel later?
- Recall a time when someone responded to your need. How did you feel about their helpfulness?

Padre Pio's Legacy

THE call to speak at a conference on Padre Pio came from Vincent Pennisi. He's a San Francisco doctor afflicted with inoperable bone cancer. I found myself wondering why this good man, so badly hurting from his disease, would want to spend time and energy celebrating a priest who died in 1968. Dr. Pennisi provided the answer himself. In times of greatest trial, he and millions of other people have found comfort and inspiration from the saintly stigmatist from Italy.

My job was to explain how Padre Pio, a Franciscan monk who carried on his body the five wounds sustained by Christ the day He was crucified, had relevance to those of us who live in the 21st century. As I read about and studied the life of this holy man, I came to realize that he continues to reflect a message we need to embrace.

1. For example, Padre Pio continuously warned people to place the spiritual world over the material world. Like Pope John Paul II, Padre Pio recognized that "things" have become the gods of our age. People have come to see riches as the ultimate purpose of life. That, he argued, was bogus. As a peasant who stayed focused on Christ, Padre Pio knew that the richest people in the world are those who let go of this world, and keep their vision on the world which never ends.

2. Padre Pio also reminded us that faith is meant to be put into action. Our love for Christ should motivate us toward concrete action on behalf of those in need. In his own case he worked for the establishment of a hospital which would serve all who came to it, regardless of their ability to pay for the care. And the medical attention they received would be the very best. This hospital, named Casa Sollievo Della Sofferenza (House for the Relief of Suffering) continues to be the best hope of the poor it serves each day.

3. Throughout his long life, Padre Pio also maintained a special and deeply respectful relationship with his parents. By his

18

example, he taught us that those who bring forth and nurture life are special gifts to us from God. They should be, he felt, treated with honor and appreciation. In an age which tries to push the elderly aside, that's a message we need now more than ever.

4. Padre Pio was also proof positive that miracles do still happen. The wounds of Christ which scarred his body from 1918 until his death were the result of a deep spiritual oneness with Christ. And what's particularly telling about the ways of God, is that he chose a simple, faithful, devoted, physically weak vessel to be an instrument of His presence.

5. Padre Pio's life testifies to the actual presence of Satan. Padre Pio spoke often of his continuous battle with the devil. In our age, we've often tried to downplay the existence of Satan, of a devil, of "the evil one," even of hell. Padre Pio, blessed with a celestial vision, was nonetheless keenly aware of the existence and the power of a darker reality. The devil, he told us, was for real.

6. Padre Pio was an extremely popular confessor. We're told that people came from around the world to celebrate the Sacrament with him. And what made him popular was not only his uncanny ability to know before words were spoken what sin had been committed; but he also strongly challenged the penitents to change their patterns of life. He could be tough, but people knew he was battling for the salvation of a soul. Sometimes, in the sacrament, I'm inclined to soft-pedal the sin, so as to offer comfort to the person confessing. Padre Pio would have none of that. He told people not always what they wanted to hear, but what they needed to hear.

7. Throughout his life, Padre Pio spoke time and time again about the value and sacredness of every human life. In that, he had terrific insight. He knew we live in an age of tremendous advancements. But we are also more adept at eliminating and denigrating the inherent value of humanity. He was, truly, a

prophet who knew that sometimes we get so filled with ourselves, we forget the true author of life is God and that only God has the right to bring life to completion.

8. Would Padre Pio have chosen to be subject to the stigmata? Of course not. He wanted only to serve the Lord as a friar. But his life also alerts us to accepting the curve balls of life. Like Mary, the mother of Jesus, Padre Pio knew that embracing the faith means that we let God lead where He chooses for us to go. That's not a surrender anyone finds easy. For Padre Pio, a private man, it meant accepting a public role for all of his adult life. It meant carrying the wounds of Christ. It meant embracing Calvary.

9. One final thought about Padre Pio. His life and ministry brought people back to the faith. He was a true evangelizer. He was a dogged battler for the Catholic Christian faith. But he made the point, again and again, that building up the Church was not simply the work of priests and Sisters. Evangelization, he said, was the responsibility of every believer. And wherever the Church is attacked or persecuted, it is our collective responsibility to stand tall in defense of our faith. Padre Pio's life was an inspiration and a lesson. He was honored by the Church with canonization on May 2, 1999. His message continues to challenge us long after his passing into eternal life.

Questions for Reflection

- How does Padre Pio's life compare with your expectations of how saints live?
- Do you think people today accept the reality of evil the way Padre Pio did? Why? Why not?

Gentle Joe Bernardin

SEVERAL years ago, I was invited to speak at a gathering of the Illinois State Catholic Conference. And while I welcomed the opportunity to address this committed group of Catholic Christians, I was especially delighted to have a chance to share a dinner with Cardinal Joseph Bernardin. He was that evening, as always, gracious, welcoming, genuinely interested in his guest and so very kind. He was also in a clearly happy personal state. As I asked him about his health, his face lit up in a full and satisfied smile. "They tell me that I'm now cancer-free," he said. This was remarkable in that his original diagnosis had been so serious. It was good to see him so happy, so relieved, and so very much at peace.

That peace was not to last. Only months later his cancer had returned with a vengeance, and this time there would be no reprieve. When he died in November 1996, Cardinal Bernardin left a vast legacy to the Catholic Church in America. Much of it was social, political and spiritual. But his greater gift was personal—because he taught us how to confront and conquer our fears.

In interviews and in writing, Cardinal Bernardin admitted that he was plagued in life by three overwhelming fears. He feared scandal. He feared cancer. And he feared death. With a deep and sensitive humanity, he overcame each of these fears. And he always gave the credit to God.

As an ambitious and talented priest, Joe Bernardin knew that he had a good chance to go far in the Church. But he also knew that the path to office was dependent on the avoidance of scandal. Reputation is key in Church leadership. How ironic then, that at the pinnacle of his success, as a Cardinal-Archbishop, he should be accused falsely of sexual impropriety. But Cardinal Bernardin being a man of integrity acted with dignity and strength. He told the world that he had never taken advantage of anyone; he wished his accuser well; and he acted without anger. He coupled his denial with the promise of prayer for all those who were victims of abuse. In time his accuser recanted. It might have ended there except for the compassion which fueled Cardinal Bernardin's goodness. He traveled to his accuser's home, prayed the Mass with him, and gave him comfort in his illness (the young man who had raised the charges was battling AIDS). He not only forgave his accuser, he poured out his love for a man for whom many would have had anger. He taught us how to forgive and to cherish those who are difficult to love.

Of his other fears, the record is clear. His father's own early death from cancer frightened Joe Bernardin. He hoped to avoid his father's end. But when it came, he fought his battle with empathy for others who waged a similar struggle. He spent long hours giving comfort to others who fought cancer, lending them hope and consolation. The cardinal never hid or denied his disease, nor did he obscure the inevitability of death. Instead he echoed the late great priest-writer Henri Nouwen in seeing death "not as an enemy but as a friend." In the face of his suffering, he managed to make his pain a teachable moment. For as the Supreme Court determines whether or not to legalize assisted suicide, Cardinal Bernardin wrote a letter to the high court encouraging them to treat all life as sacred. And he used his own struggle as witness against the use of pain as a rationale for terminating the terminally ill. He spoke not as a churchman, but as a person about to die who nonetheless saw the value and beauty even of limited or pain-filled life.

On a personal level, I will admit to reservations about this noble man when we first became acquainted. He was the proponent of an approach to life called "the consistent ethic," or "seamless garment." It recognized the value of all life, born and unborn. It argues that we have a moral obligation to be defenders not only of innocent life, but of every living creature, good or bad. At first I worried that this approach might diminish the force of our anti-abortion efforts. Now I recognize that consistency only fuels and empowers all we hope to accomplish. It lends us a moral credibility of unimpeachable value.

Some journals of the left and right have attempted to categorize Cardinal Joseph Bernardin. Liberals want to claim him as their own; conservatives are quick to let them have him. Truth be told he was a person of no ideological extreme. He was, instead, a man of deep goodness, who served God best in loving His people. He taught us to face our fears with courage, with class and with faith. Was he a saint? I don't know. But if you page through Butler's *Lives of the Saints*, you'll surely find many like Joe Bernardin: fully human, fully alive, struggling with life's disappointments and pains, slow to judge others, quick to forgive, longing to bring home the person who's hardest to love. We're all richer for having shared these times with gentle Joe Bernardin.

Question for Reflection

● What qualities did Cardinal Bernardin possess which helped him to overcome false accusations and to face his cancer valiantly and still remain a gentle man?

Mary's Meaning

THERE'S an interesting phenomenon developing not only in America, but across the globe. Youth conferences, which years ago would have focused on issues like sexuality or communication skills or family systems or drugs or alcohol, have been joined by a new approach to an old reality. There are now conventions and conferences aimed at teaching teens and young adults about the messages of Mary, the mother of Jesus. And, of course, that makes a lot of sense because as a role model for young people, Mary really has it all. Consider the components of her life:

—She was probably a teenager herself when asked to be the mother of God. It was not what she had planned for herself. She was engaged to Joseph and might well have expected a traditional role as wife and mother. Instead, the angel Gabriel asked much more of her. Her response of "be it done unto me according to your will" was an act of both courage and faith. She has an awesome trust in God and placed her entire life in the hands of the Almighty.

—Saying yes to God didn't promise her an easy ride. No, she was still subject to trials, tribulations, confusing times and moments of intense personal pain. And just as young people today feel the inviting if misleading temptation to go with what's popular at the expense of what has value, Mary stayed faithful even when some people (like Herod) tried to kill her son. Or when she was asked (shortly after her child was born) to flee to Egypt. Can you imagine what a tough trip that must have been 2,000 years ago?

—Mary was also a person of profound humility. You'd think that becoming the mother of God might make you cocky or haughty or proud. I mean, look at some of the outrageously self-centered things singers and actors say about themselves today when they get their five minutes of fame! And yet, Mary never acted that way. She seemed to know that everything we are, everything we have, is a gift from God. She seemed to understand that all is grace, that we are not our own creators, but that we co-create our lives with God. That knowledge gave Mary a deep sense of rootedness. She didn't let her specialness inflate her ego or make her think she was better than others.

—Mary also taught us what truly matters. Many young people, as they pass through adolescence, seem to feel they can discard their families. Friends and schoolmates become more important than the people we grew up with. Brothers and sisters start to be replaced by our peers. That never seemed to happen to Mary. She always put her family first. She always seemed to recognize that while people and friendships come and go, our families can be forever if we just commit ourselves to making them work. I'm sure that like any family, they had their ups and downs; but Mary, Joseph and Jesus could always count on each other.

—I notice, too, that many of my teen-age friends allow their personal problems to overwhelm them, so that their lives become entirely centered on the particular crisis they face at any given moment. There'll be hours on the phone sorting out the latest relational mishap or moods which shift from day to day owing to the successes or failures we experience at school. And sometimes our daily problems can just overwhelm us. Mary taught us a way out of this kind of paralysis, this kind of self-absorption. When she found out she was pregnant, she might easily have spent months on herself. She could easily have fallen victim to the "why me?" syndrome. But she didn't. Instead, Mary gets up and travels across the rocky hill country of Judea (walking it, by the way) to visit with and help her elder cousin Elizabeth, who is also expecting a baby. In other words, she found that giving to someone else in need was the best response to the challenges we all face. You can either be selfless or selfish. And Mary knew that giving and serving the needs of others was a positive way out of the useless quagmire

of self-pity. Mary has so much to teach us about living and loving. It's no wonder that young people around the world are
rediscovering her amazing and important life. Pick up the
Bible again. Look up the chapters on the life of this centered
and solid teen-age woman. And see in her story the way to a
life fully realized.

Questions for Reflection

● Remembering that Mary faced the same challenges and
  fears as teenagers today can help parents and their young
  adults. Write her a letter or poem identifying your concerns
  and confusions.

● Now let her speak to your heart.

Cardinal Basil Hume: Healer

IN 1976, Pope Paul VI did something rather surprising. Examining a vacancy in the Archdiocese of Westminster, England, he bypassed all the bishops who might have expected to be named Primate of England. Instead he chose a Benedictine monk, an Abbott from the Ampleforth Monastery. It was an inspired choice. Evidence of its wisdom surfaced some years later when a survey of English opinion indicated that this Catholic archbishop was the most respected and highly esteemed spiritual leader in the country. That's especially remarkable when you consider that Catholics are a small minority in England, and that there is a rich history of animosity between Catholics and Anglicans going back to Henry VIII. Cardinal Basil Hume bridged the differences with kindness, humility and wisdom. His death on June 17, 1999 of cancer leaves a great void, but also the memory of a man, a person of the Church whom we might well model and emulate.

I first met Cardinal Hume in 1980. Two years before I had taken the chance of asking him to visit New York and speak at a charity for disabled children. Frankly, I didn't expect him to accept. He not only came to help the children but gave a talk of insight and grace. He told us that "special" children give us a window into the heart of God. Rather than viewing challenged children as a burden, Cardinal Hume encouraged us to see them as a privilege and blessing. I remember one mother of a seriously retarded child leaving the talk with tears in her eyes: she felt ennobled by a Prince of the Church who recognized the particular beauty and value of the son others would pity.

Throughout the years, I've had the privilege of enjoying the friendship and support of this noble man. Several years ago he made a point of making the time during a summer sojourn in America to tape an extended interview for our television program. It was an experience which illuminated the uniqueness of this good man. He never moved away from Church teach-

ing, but presented his adherence with understanding, com-
mon-sense clarity and a self-evident compassion. On the right
to life, for example, Cardinal Hume explained that he believed
in the protection of all life not only because of Church teaching.
He explained that he'd sought out medical doctors to explain
to him, in detail, the process of conception and fetal development. Through their tutelage he came to recognize both med-
ically and morally that life, from its inception, was precious
and worthy of defense.

In many ways, I think Cardinal Hume was precisely the
kind of leader needed by our Church. He was, without exception, faithful to the Magisterium. But he also recognized that
too many people walk away from the Church's teachings when
they're presented without a human and compassionate face. So
he allowed for this resistance. He never condoned it, but he
understood it. He never agreed with those who rejected
Church teaching, but he always let them know they were
loved. "We can disagree," he once told me, "but we must never
stop loving each other." That notion extended itself to those
who practiced birth control, to those who supported the death
penalty, to those living a sexual life at odds with the Church's
wisdom, to those who supported wars the Church viewed as
unjust, and to those who condoned racism. He stated the truth,
but always tempered it with understanding and affection.
Some (including the writer of his obituary in The New York
Times) saw this as weakness or waffling. They judged him
unfairly. And in assessing him that way they forgot that
Cardinal Hume's faith was built around a Man who, when
confronted with an adulterous woman, responded with truth,
challenge, forgiveness and unconditional love.

In an age when some conservatives would give in to judgment and condemnation towards those who do not "toe the
line" on Church doctrine, while any number of liberals would
dismiss the same teaching as hierarchical and therefore worthy

of scorn, Cardinal Hume represented the middle way. He embraced the teaching, but recognized and was willing to work with our imperfect human condition. I suppose you'd call him a Church moderate. And he would view that as a compliment.

When, in 1998, Cardinal Hume reached the mandatory retirement age of 75, he happily sent his letter of resignation to Pope John Paul II. He spoke of returning to life at the Abbey. Not surprising, the Holy Father rejected his resignation and asked him to continue in office. That affirmation was, I believe, the Pope's recognition of Basil Hume's special gift for our Church. In a highly secularized society, he helped people to focus on the things of God. In a culture given to constant compromises of human life, he argued for letting people live. In a world given too easily to war and retribution he asked for the use of restraint and reason. In a society in which sex became as meaningless as a handshake, he spoke of the divine and joyous nature of committed human sexual loving. And in a world (and Church) too given to polarization, he worked mightily to bring us together. When I meet a person of the Church, I often ask myself a simple question: could I imagine going to confession to this person? I could (and did) see in this cardinal-archbishop someone who was first and always a priest, a man of faith, someone who'd always tell you the truth, but always with tenderness, gentleness and compassion.

Basil Cardinal Hume, O.S.B., a gentle soul, a wise teacher, a compassionate healer, may he rest in his well-earned peace.

Questions for Reflection

- Imagine yourself going to confession to this wise and compassionate healer. What areas of your life would you bring up to Cardinal Hume?
- What is the truth you hear him speaking tenderly and gently?

John the Hero

THROUGHOUT the season of Advent, anyone going to church is going to hear a lot about John the Baptist. As the herald or "announcer" for the coming of Jesus Christ, John's a frequent character in the pre-Christmas Gospel.

You might wonder what relevance John has to us in contemporary America. I think his meaning and his message are absolutely relevant to the way we lead our lives and choices we make everyday. Let me give some examples of what I mean:

1) John the Baptist chose to live simply, to be free of the earthly possessions that oftentimes own us. We're told he owned only what he wore, ate simply, and was a man without a permanent home. In this, I think John is reminding us that our culture tells us time and time again that things and possessions will make us happy and that our culture is wrong. You can live in the grandest house, drive the best car, wear the finest clothes, smell of the most expensive perfumes, belong to the elitist clubs, and still feel a hollowness in your soul. Knowing that, John called on us to renounce the myth that things give life meaning. Instead, he'd tell us that spiritual wholeness is the only true source of fulfillment.

One year, when a "Furby" was the hottest toy out there, I spent long hours trying to find one for my niece and nephew. Everyone wanted one and the stores couldn't produce them quickly enough. There was literally a sense of "Furby madness" as otherwise rational adults strove to obtain the one item that would satisfy their demanding children.

Recently, while walking through my young nephew's bedroom, I saw last year's rage lying in a pile of other discarded toys and gifts. For all the fuss and bother, Furby was one more promise of happiness which faded as the latest trend. Take a Furby and multiply it by a thousand, because that's the number of times we'll probably buy into the concept that some item, some thing, will bring us true joy. Of course, it never really does.

2) St. John the Baptist also taught us to speak our own truth. One thing you can't deny about John is his willingness to march to the beat of his own drummer. He doesn't follow crowds or trends. He walks a path that is uniquely his own. And he refuses to remain silent.

What a stark contrast that offers to the lives we lead. At work, regardless of the oppression we often feel from bosses and supervisors, we remain silent. Early on, we buy into the concept that silence will "keep us out of trouble."

At home, it's more of the same. I wish I had a dollar for every wife who told me that she goes along to get along—that disagreeing with her husband will only make matters worse. In the same way, I've seen whole families act as if their alcoholic mother isn't really drunk. There's a sense that if we make believe it isn't really happening, then maybe the problem will cease to exist. Of course it only stays and grows worse. Our silence enables the problem to expand and move forward unchecked.

Our silence extends to matters of public policy too. American Catholics make up over 25 percent of the population, but matter relatively little politically. Our Jewish brothers and sisters, on the other hand, constitute only 3% of the general population, but have a far greater impact on the issues that matter to them. Why? Because like John the Baptist, they're not afraid to share the truth with others.

3) St. John was also a man who was comfortable with who he was, and with who he was not. Imagine his situation. Thousands of people came to him, honored him, lauded and followed him. He was a charismatic star in many ways. Not a few people would have loved for him to own the spotlight and

declare himself to be "the man," the Messiah, the King. But he knows better. He uses his notoriety to focus on Christ. He deflects the attention and adulation to someone he honors, his Lord. That's not easy to do. We all have inclinations to believe that we're important, that we are who people want us to be.

Today, I fear, we often conform ourselves to become an image of what society wants us to be. He knew who he was. He understood his inherent value as a child of God. But he also knew who he was not. His message for you and me: Be true to yourself. Don't live to please others, and don't become what others expect. Be able to look in the mirror and like the real person you are. John did that, and it's one of the reasons we still celebrate his life.

4) One final reason to highlight John the Baptist: he had the courage of his convictions. He was willing to put himself at risk for a higher value. He wasn't "politically correct" in the ways of his time or culture. And for that he ultimately faced martyrdom. But I think we can be certain that the man beheaded by King Herod enjoyed a hero's welcome when he stood before his God in heaven.

In so many ways, St. John the Baptist was a man for all seasons, as relevant to our lives as any biblical figure you're likely to find.

Questions for Reflection

- John was independent and confident in himself but he was a man for others. How did he learn and maintain this life stance?

- Which people and places are your guiding stars?

Gospel Jewels

THE word "gospel" means "good news." The Christmas season is rich in stories which inspire and give hope. It's a season which seems to highlight our better selves. Two recent stories come to mind.

Patrick Erickson is a remarkable man. He's raised a large and value-centered family with his loving wife of fifty years, Jean Marie. His commitment to Catholic Christian values is unbending. He's surely the most pro-life witness I've ever met, putting most of us to shame by his unyielding dedication. Pat has prayed for years outside an abortion center. As a witness to life, he's been punched out, spit on and cursed, repeatedly. He goes back anyway, smiles at those who hate him, loves those who disagree with him and prays for women in crisis pregnancies.

Recently, Pat became seriously ill with a brain tumor and a follow-up stroke. For months he hung on the brink, brought back by the love and care of many, especially his Jean Marie. On Christmas day, Jean found herself driving to the hospital to see Pat. Being focused on him for all his months of infirmity, she never checked her gas gauge. Sure enough, alone on a deserted parkway, her car died for lack of gasoline. Car after car winged by, no one stopping to see what this senior citizen needed. All the folks caught up in a hurry to celebrate. Finally, a car stopped. Out stepped two men, one black, the other Hispanic. Jean Marie and her family are just about as white as people can be. She needed help but was just a little concerned. She needn't have been. These two men, sizing up the problem went off to a gas station several miles away to obtain the necessary gas. They couldn't get it because they had no container. So they drove back to Jean Marie and offered to push her car with theirs into the nearest gas station. Once there, they filled her gas tank. When Jean Marie made an effort to reimburse the men, they politely declined. One explained: "With all this fuss about Christmas, I never really felt it until now. Thank you for letting us help. Merry Christmas, Jean Marie." And with that, these, guardian angels disappeared.

Another hidden Gospel jewel comes to mind. Edward Raber, husband to Mary, father to five, grandfather and great-grandfather, returned to God on New Year's Day. Ed was a faith-filled, loving and wise gentleman. In so many ways, he reflected the true vocation of Christian living. But, I discovered, he did his best Christian living quietly and without recognition. On the Thursday after his burial, I was having dinner with a priest friend, Father Simon Pai. He noted Ed Raber's passing with special regret. I was surprised to know he even knew Ed, and so he told me how. Seems Father Simon was helping out in Ed Raber's parish, and shared with the people there the story of his brother and the struggles of living in China. He shared with Ed and those listening, a story of the special value Simon's brother placed on a bicycle he'd been given eighteen years before. It was a prized and treasured means of transportation. Simon's point was that people in need often have greater appreciation than we who are so richly blessed. Ed. Raber was moved by this story. He pondered it in his heart. Now, you should know that Ed Raber was not in any way a rich man. He worked hard throughout his life, did without for the sake of his children, and lived simply. But something of the image of people in need in a faraway place struck a chord in his heart. And he wanted to make a small difference for the good.

Next week at Mass, Ed Raber quietly approached Father Simon. He slipped him an envelope and asked him to share it with his brother in China. Father Simon was later shocked to discover that the envelope contained $2,000.

People Ed Raber would never meet, never directly experience, benefited from the deep and caring generosity of a vital Christian heart.

All around us are Gospel jewels, stories of goodness and compassion, stories of empathy and generosity. It's easy at times to write the world off as jaded and hopeless. Don't you believe it. It's still God's world and sometimes we do shine!

Questions for Reflection

● Spend a few moments thanking God for the remarkable Christians—like Ed and Pat—that you know. What do they have in common?

● Which gifts do you recognize as your own?

Being Truly Prepared

WHEN I was visiting a class of students in our parish school during Advent, we got into a discussion about the meaning of the season. When pressed for its meaning, most came up with the key concept: a time of preparation. But preparation for what? Ah, that was easy for most every one. It's preparation time for Christmas? That's true, but it's not really complete. Yes, Advent has been a time to become prepared for the birth of Jesus. But it's also significantly more. This season doesn't just challenge us to meet the Christ child on December 25th. Its more important purpose is to ascertain our readiness to meet Him at the time of life's closure. It's been a season to examine our life's purpose, our reason for being here, our success or failure in making a difference for the good. Christmas has meaning in direct proportion to our ability to look in the mirror and say "I've lived a wonderful life, because I've tried to live it for others."

Sometimes examples help the point. Several years ago three New York City firefighters died in a heroic effort to save the lives of elderly and infirm residents in a retirement home. Joseph Cavalieri, James Bohan and Christopher Bopp will be remembered as champions of life and love forever. They paid the ultimate price in a selfless act of goodness a week before Christmas. But they also accomplished much more. By all accounts, these guys were all-around great and giving men who lived lives of charity and concern for others. Through acts of kindness and compassion they were well prepared for the coming of Christmas. One known for individual acts of thoughtfulness, helping other people who were down on their luck. Another liked to play Santa Claus for kids, bringing smiles and joy to the little ones. The other was an organizer, who worked in this season to see that toys were collected for children who might not otherwise enjoy a merry Christmas. All were Catholic Christians who seemed to recognize that preparation for the holiday we call Christmas is really a dress rehearsal for our most significant encounter with the child whose birthday we celebrate, the Messiah, the Redeemer, the Holy One of God. By that standard, Joseph and James and Christopher are probably having the fullest expression of Christmas right now: living in the loving embrace of a Jesus who tells them "well done, good and faithful friends, come and enter the Kingdom which has been prepared for you."

None of these men knew that their lives would end that day. They were just doing their jobs, like thousands of their compatriots. But from what we know of their personal lives, they were also deeply prepared for an encounter with Christ because they lived His compassion in truly authentic ways. Never let anyone tell you that the world doesn't have heroes anymore. Joseph, James and Christopher are such heroes, and not just for what they did in that tragic fire, but for how they lived their lives.

A final word about Christmas. With the world brightly lit and joyously festive music everywhere, we're certainly right in expecting people to be filled with gladness. So why isn't it always so? As a priest, I hear from more people who are depressed or anxious, lonely or troubled at this time of the year than any other time of the year. Maybe it has to do with false expectations. With everyone telling you that this is a season of happiness we can sometimes look at our own lives and ponder the failures more that the successes. But "the blues" don't have to be overwhelming. People like you and me can help. A timely call, a special note, a surprise visit to cheer and to express love can be an incredible tonic. So, in addition to the wrapped gifts and the many-mailed cards, in addition to the lively decorations and well-cooked meal, why not think about that fellow spending Christmas alone? Or the woman down the street who's just come through a stinging divorce? Or the widower who had lots of people to care during the wake but is now left in the downward spiral of Christmas with too many memories? Or how about that family who has the child with special physical challenges, couldn't they use a little extra encouragement? Or what about the priest you'll listen to on Christmas morning whose parents are gone and who's got no wife or kids to share the holiday with, would he be spending the day alone in a rectory? Or the people next door who got that notice two weeks ago that they're not needed at work anymore, "downsizing," doing it's dirty best. Couldn't our abundance help make their lack a little less intense?

We've got the power to make it a brighter Christmas. Let's not walk on by!

Questions for Reflection

- What can you do "to keep Christmas in your heart all year"?
- How will it change the way you do things?

Leading Others

A S a guest of Fox News, I was recently asked what the most damaging effects of President Clinton's indiscretions might be. Most of the discussion had centered on his legal and political difficulties. I moved the discussion in a different direction. His greatest problem wasn't about the law; it was and is about setting the wrong example. My fear is the message his behavior probably sends to young people about reverence for the gift of human sexuality. He has so much power: to lead, to direct, to focus, to encourage. And young people are so susceptible to the right kinds of example. I sure hope Mr. Clinton uses his remaining time in office to lead others down a different road from the one he's personally followed.

Example means more than we realize. And young people are such sponges. Even when we think they're not listening or noticing, they're taking it all in. That became clear to me during conversations on our "Personally Speaking" television interview program. I asked my guests about the role models who helped them to embrace faith and morality. Without exception, every guest had been led by others to the good lives they now embrace. A few examples help to make the point.

Mary Cunningham Agee heads The Nurturing Network, an organization that offers alternatives to young women who experience a crisis pregnancy. The inspiration for the network is Mary's faith, a faith she learned as a child from her uncle, a priest. In the absence of a father (he had deserted the family), her uncle taught her about our loving and unconditionally supportive Father in Heaven. That image of a loving and protective God helped Mary Agee to see that real faith offers help and protection to the needy. That understanding of life's meaning came from the example of her uncle.

Bill Baker was also a guest. He's the president of PBS, a powerful person in the world of American television. And yet he still has his priorities straight. God, experienced through regular prayer and attendance at Mass, his marriage vows and his role as a parent are the central issues of his life. And who helped Dr. Baker to recognize what "really matters?" His wife of three decades, Jean-Marie. Whenever he decided that important secular matters needed to be the center of his life, a voice called him back: the steady, consistent and loving voice of a wife and mother who has her priorities clear. He calls her "the church Lady," but says it with admiration and love.

David Campbell is a popular singer, now setting new records in the New York cabaret scene. His albums are selling like wildfire. On the show he demonstrated perhaps his greatest gift: not only does he have a beautiful voice, he also possesses a positive, affirming and loving spirit. And where does that love of life and others come from? David told us that he was conceived during a one-night stand. When he was born his mother handed him over to his grandmother. His biological Mom was only 17 when he was born. And yet he never felt deprived, never wanted for love, always felt appreciated and always felt special. How come? Because his grandmother always treated him as if he were a gift. Her love, her total acceptance of him as a gift from above made him believe in the absolute goodness of life and love. His sense of himself, of his inherent worth, came from a parent figure who always made him aware of his special place in her heart. Her example made him the man he is today.

When Cardinal William Keeler of Baltimore and Archbishop John Foley of the Holy See were guests, I asked them the question you always ask a priest. So, who influenced you to choose priesthood? Both testified to the great love for God and the Church given to them by parents who delighted in their faith. They passed that delight and the understanding that faith should be put concretely into action by serving others, to their sons. And look how parental example has blessed the Church!

Bishop Patrick Ahern says his inspiration was, typically, a family of faith. But he was also inspired by a friend who wondered aloud "if you're so very Catholic, how come you only get to Church on Sundays? Why not go every day?" He realized the friend was right and started attending daily Mass on a regular basis. The Eucharist helped him recognize the call he had in his heart to serve others as a priest. In tough times, when he doubted his vocation, he had another inspiration—St. Therese, the Little Flower. He read her autobiography and realized from her simplicity and humanity that even in his fragile human nature, he could serve the Lord very well indeed. Bishop Ahern has tried to share the help he got from St. Therese with others by writing a book called *Maurice and Therese*. She inspired him to be a priest, and now Bishop Ahern hopes to share her special witness with others.

Every one of my guests tells a story about people who touched him or her, offered a witness to emulate. Every one of us is a compilation of the people who form us, nurture us, guide us and inspire us by their examples. People, especially the young, are watching you and me right now. What's the testimony of our lives telling them? Is it leading them closer to the things of Christ, or placing distance between them and the source of everything that truly matters?

Questions for Reflection

- Use the last paragraph of this essay to reflect on how others are being influenced by your actions. What encourages you to make a difference?
- What discourages you from trying?

Part II

Life Issues

Words and Meanings

WE'VE all been through the joys and pains of standardized testing. From IQ tests in grade school, SAT's in High School to GRE's in Graduate School, we learn of our strengths and deficiencies. I know mine well. My math scores tell me that I better keep a calculator close at hand, and a talented accountant as my close friend. My verbal scores, by contrast, tell me that my reading and writing teachers during those early formative years did their job very well. So, for me, words matter a lot. And when I write, I try to be abundantly clear and to the point. In turn, I expect people to read me accurately.

Over the years I've expressed my vehement opposition to the death penalty. I've expressed my serious reservations about American military interventions in place like Kuwait and Bosnia. I've expressed opposition for our government's racist activities. I've argued for the rights of homosexual persons to be treated with dignity and respect. I've strongly condemned the so-called "Welfare Reform" which leaves too many of our nation's poor uncared for. I've enthusiastically argued the case for a program of universal medical coverage (while insisting that it should not include funding for abortion). I've endorsed increases in the minimum wage, supported the right to collective bargaining, and castigated the consumerist bent of capitalist society. I abhor the tragedy of gun violence in America, and strongly support greater controls, I've also written of my involvement in the anti-war movement and specifically, the war in Vietnam. How, I'm left wondering, can a person with such positions be dismissed as someone "in love with the Republican Party." These are not, for the record, positions widely held in the GOP.

As far as support for Republican candidates, I've liked some while decisively dismissing others. That included local Republican Congressmen, presidential candidates like Pat Buchanan, Governors like George Pataki and the pro-choice militancy of Mayor Rudolph Guiliani. On the opposite side of the aisle, I've written glowingly of Democrats like Senator Eugene McCarthy (whose anti-war presidential campaign I had the privilege to assist), Governor Robert Casey of Pennsylvania for his dedication to a consistent ethic of life, Congressmen Gene Taylor and Tom Manton for being true profiles of courage, and Mayor Ed Koch and Senator Daniel Patrick Moynihan for their wise opposition to the butchery of partial birth abortion.

In other words, a person's political party means precious little. It's the positions and policies they hold. Uniformly or uncritically supporting a person or party makes no sense for the individual trying to reflect a Christian conscience. Instead, I'd suggest the candidates of any party should be evaluated on the basis of the values they not only espouse in word but in deed.

The Church gives a basic means for judgment and it revolves around a politician's willingness to embrace the so-called "Seamless Garment." This will involve a desire by that candidate or office holder to support laws which protect and defend human life at every stage of our development from conception to actual death. So then, we cannot easily choose to vote for candidates who would forfeit the rights of pre-born children. Neither can we ever embrace a candidate who uses a platform of racial division to advance his or her cause. And those who seek electoral success by clamoring for capital punishment do not reflect an appreciation for the sovereignty of God's dominion over human life, and should be challenged for their advance of the "culture of death." We are the keepers of our sisters and brothers, even more acutely when they are poor, unemployed, marginalized and powerless. Those who would demonize the new American immigrants because they don't look European are promoting a racist view of our country which is unacceptable for the Catholic conscience. And with all due respect to the Bill of Rights, it's unlikely the

Founding Fathers of our nation had the weapons we now use to exploit and destroy lives in mind when they wrote in defense of our right to bear arms. In these issues, and in all evaluations of those who seek government office, there is one steady measure of evaluation: do they support or undermine the lives of the community?

Sometimes we pro-lifers are criticized for being "single issue." Those, even in the Church, who would seek to trivialize us, suggest that we care only for the unborn child. In truth, pro-lifers and Catholic Christians in general, are asked to use the affirmation of human life as a mode for accurately judging the worthiness of any candidate to hold office. And, here it gets dicey—for we cannot trade away one class of human life for another. Life isn't negotiable currency. So, for example, the candidate who supports gun control but promotes the abortion of children is not an acceptable choice for us—anymore than a candidate who supports the pre-born, but cuts off aid to dependent children. Instead, our purpose as Catholics attempting to make our values known must focus on those who support and defend all human life. The problem: neither major party does it with any consistency. So we must, candidate by candidate, choose wisely and carefully.

I do not support all Republicans because some are simply wrong on the issues. Likewise, I cannot support any number of Democrats who are wrong on the issues. And what issues do I mean? Those issues in which a candidate fails to articulate a true belief in the sanctity of every human life.

Questions for Reflection

- What rule of thumb do you use to choose between candidates on an issue?
- Do you believe that your opposition/support of a candidate makes a difference? Why? Why not?

Intolerance

TWO newspapers regularly arrive on my desk at about the same time. One is called The Wanderer, and it offers the view of very conservative people in the Catholic Church. Next to it lies the National Catholic Reporter, offering an extremely liberal perspective on what's happening in the Church. I read both with interest and dismay. In each paper, the news is slanted to the ideological perspective of the publishers. But more troubling, each sees people who hold a different point of view as almost "the enemy." I suspect that the truth about our Church lies somewhere between these two journalistic enterprises.

Tolerance is a gift I'm finding in short supply throughout the Church. As we become more entrenched in the rightness of our positions (on either the left or right), we seem to shut off the possibility that there is truth on both sides of the fence. Let me offer a few of the experiences of intolerance I've personally experienced.

"Humanae Vitae" is, in some sectors of the Church, a litmus test for ideological purity. If you support the Holy Father's stance on the wrongness of artificial contraception (and I do), you are viewed as a true Catholic. When I was appointed to my position as family life director, there were some in the conservative camp who questioned my dedication to this teaching. That's fine, and they have every right to question me about my viewpoint. One woman, however, went too far. And she represents the intolerance I think ultimately hurts our community immensely.

I was sitting one Saturday afternoon in the confessional box. Someone came in to talk about her marriage. She broached the topic of birth control. She asked a number of highly pointed questions about the teaching, suggesting that it was a problem in her marriage. I answered to the best of my ability but did wonder why she was going into such interrogative detail. Then

47

I heard a suspicious sound, the hum of small machinery. With hopes that I was wrong in my assumption, I got up and walked out of my section of the confessional box and pulled back the curtain on hers. Sure enough, I found a woman equipped with a hand-held tape recorder. She'd been taping our conversation in the obvious hope that I'd say something heretical.

There are few times I can ever remember being as angry. Not at what this person was attempting to do to me, but at what she was actually doing to the Sacrament of Reconciliation. My words were, I think, to the point: "Ma'am, people like you think you're defending the Church, believe that you stand with the Pope. But, in fact, you're violating him, the Church and everything decent. Please leave." With a look of embarrassment, the woman left, tape securely in hand. In the name of orthodoxy, she had committed a serious wrong. She had allowed her intolerance to supersede her judgment.

I don't want to suggest that this misguided person represents conservatives in the Church, because she doesn't. But she does represent a troubling minority whose lack of respect for other viewpoints causes, I believe, deep wounds to the body of Christ. Nor are these intolerances limited to those on the right. I find some self-styled liberals to be just as rigid, just as intolerant in their progressive orthodoxy.

Another example comes to mind. In the battle against the reinstatement of the death penalty, I've had the chance to work long and hard hours with a number of people from liberal organizations. In one case, I worked closely with a lawyer who did incredible work in this futile cause. When I asked her why she did it, she replied, "Because if we can't protect the people who are the lowest of the low, then we're compromising all life." An answer I obviously loved. So I asked my new co-worker to join me in an upcoming public witness against abortion. Her face clouded over, and she demurred with words which haunt, "That, Jim, is a private matter. I don't want to touch the abortion thing." What fraudulence! How can all life be sacred in one instance, but not in the case of pre-born children? Sadly, that's a common experience I have with folks who operate the social justice machinery of the Church. They say all the right things about life, but won't lift a finger to defend the unborn. In their quiet minds, they think of us as zealots, extremists, or worse. And all because we think that developing children have a birth right.

There is a frightening condescension among folks in the far reaches of both the liberal and conservative camps. Both can see the other in extremist tones. It's time, I think, to turn the bombast down. To see with eyes of tolerance. To judge a little less severely. Truth doesn't have a side or a camp. It travels, like the Spirit, within the hearts and minds and souls of all who believe.

Question for Reflection

- How does the Eucharistic tradition of "everyone being invited to share at the table" influence your openness to those who have differing views?

Why Bother?

DURING the eleven years I served as a diocesan pro-life director, my friends often asked me, "why bother?" From their perspective the issue looks to be a dead-end. Politically, pro-life forces face an uphill battle. Judicially, there are similar roadblocks. The American populace, while deeply uncomfortable with the horror of abortion, seems unwilling to radically change this tragic situation. So where, then, do we draw hope? Why continue to fight? Why not just give up? Let me offer just one reason. One vital human life.

Over two years ago I was out preaching at a church in Selden. Following my homily on abortion, a nervous young woman approached me. She was, she told me, pregnant and unmarried. No one in her family wanted her to have this child. She was not in a favorable financial situation and the father of her baby was not especially thrilled to be a Dad. We talked. I must tell you that I did not think I convinced her to have her baby. Sometimes you can just sense that the person is going to abort. That was the feeling I got. But then a letter arrived from that young woman. Let me share with you what Joanne wrote: "I hope you remember me. We met in January of last year at St. Margaret of Scotland Church in Selden, N.Y. You were giving a homily based on abortion. I came to you to ask for your help, as far as my pregnancy went, and you were happy to give it to me.

"Believe me, that time in my life was the most difficult time I've ever experienced. No one was on my side until I met you. You gave me hope and allowed me to believe in myself and my baby. After I saw you on the altar I began to develop courage. And at the same time you put the fear of God back into my life. I realized that God had always been with me and I was just neglecting to see him. You helped me realize that, and I believe that you were the answer to the prayer I was praying. You were the miracle I was asking for.

"Now, one year later, I have a beautiful son, Christopher Joseph. And all the fears I had are replaced with happiness. No other child that I would have in the future could replace Christopher in my heart. He is a true angel who gives me no trouble at all. I thank God every time he smiles, cries, and breathes. And I thank you for helping me realize that that is all that counts.

"Before you came along, I had no faith my life could continue with a child. I felt my future was over and welfare was close at hand. I thought I would be all alone without a family and without friends who would all pass me by in life. I thought my son would grow up without a father and blame me for it. Now I know it was all untrue. Everyone loved me but they were all afraid themselves. They were afraid a baby would ruin my life and take me away from them. I thought telling my father about my pregnancy would hurt him the most. At first it did hurt, but every time he sees Christopher in the morning both of their faces light up with happiness and I realized he loves Chris as much as he loves me.

"When my family realized that my decision about keeping my baby was final, they slowly began to support me. I was prepared for the worst, though, with the programs you referred me to. These people, who didn't even know me, were willing to help me—that also gave me hope. Eventually, I convinced my son's father to stick it out with me, and as we spent more time together I realized he was just as afraid as everyone else. Now we're back together preparing a future for our new family and considering marriage. And although we are not getting married for the baby's sake, we agreed that without Christopher we could have never come together. Abortion would have only torn us apart.

"I began taking classes in January at the Community College in Selden, and in the fall I will transfer full time to Stony Brook University where I will seek a B.A. in English, and then work my way through the law school of my choice.

"Thank you, Msgr. Jim Lisante, for your kind words and support. That's all I needed from someone, and you were the one to give it to me. I'd like you to meet one of the lives that you've saved through your mission and pray that you get to many more young women like myself. If I can help in any way, Please don't hesitate to ask. Thanks again."

Whenever I think that this ministry is too frustrating; whenever I'm inclined to give up; whenever I'm tempted to shut up about the senselessness of abortion; I know what I've got to do. I'll just take out Christopher's picture, and in those wondrous eyes, I'll discover the meaning of life once again.

Questions for Reflection

- Even Jesus needed the support of friends and family to keep up the good fight. What were the words spoken to you that gave you the jolt you needed to continue?
- Who needs to hear from you right now?

For Ana Rosa

A YOUNG woman was eight months pregnant, and filled with anxiety about the expected child. The mother spoke no English, had little money and felt almost no emotional support. She did not think she could effectively mother a baby. So she went to a New York City abortion clinic run by Dr. Abu Hayat. The doctor took the mother's money and performed the abortion. He expressed no scruples, no reservations about terminating an eight-month-old baby, a child who was already viable (able to live outside the womb). But Dr. Hayat wasn't much of an abortionist. He did a botched job and only removed the unborn baby's right arm. Fearing that his discomfort might be showing, Dr. Hayat told the mother that the abortion was over and that she could leave. During that night, however, something unusual occurred. Because during that same evening the pregnant woman went into labor and delivered a beautiful little girl. A child now named Ana Rosa. She was perfect in every way save one. She had no right arm.

What happened to Ana Rosa was not unique. Over 200,000 children are aborted each year during the fifth, sixth, seventh, eighth and ninth months of pregnancy. And it's completely legal under two Supreme Court decisions (Roe vs. Wade and Doe vs. Bolton). Little people like Ana Rosa have no *right* to be born. Under our existing laws they are not considered persons,they are only seen as property which can be disposed of at will. The battle over unlimited abortion is sometimes seen as something adults pretty much dominate. But I've started asking teen-agers and young adults to think about becoming more directly involved in saving people like Ana Rosa. Consider this fact: since January 22, 1973, there are 33 million teenagers and young adults who we will never have the chance to know, to become friends with, to work with, to benefit from as brothers and sisters. The death of these people should trouble us all, because every one of us matters immensely. We are each diminished when a life is lost.

But what can you do? After all, what can one teenager or one young adult do to change a world where children like Ana Rosa are wiped out over 4,000 times a day? Well, you can speak up. Over a million teenagers will become pregnant this year in our country. Most of these young women will go into almost immediate panic. They might well include your sister, your neighbor, your best friend; they might even include you. When someone tells us they think they're pregnant we can offer one of several responses. We can cut and run, offering them little or no support. We can encourage them to "get rid of it," to abort their baby. Or we can be a life-affirming friend and explain that what's growing inside them is a person, a baby, a human life just like yours and mine, only smaller. And we can promise them that they won't have to go through it alone, that we will be there for them. That's what a true friend would do.

We can also speak up to the politicians. They do listen. Tell them (on the phone, through the mail, e-mail, or in person) that you don't think the violence of abortion makes any sense. Tell them you consider abortion of children like Ana Rosa a form of butchery. Tell them you resent having your hard-earned tax money used to pay for other people's abortions. Let them know that while you may be young, you aren't insensitive to the loss of over 33 million innocent young lives.

Questions for Reflection

- Practice what you would do and say if a friend of yours was contemplating an abortion.
- Can you commit yourself to a daily prayer to end abortion?

Meeting Sarah Smith

LIFE Forum is an educational conference held for the people of Wisconsin. Many of those who attend aren't particularly convinced about the pro-life message. But they come to learn; they come to hear another side. Like many Americans, they seek to find some area of common ground in this often divisive moral/ethical debate.

My presentation at the conference dealt with issues of the so-called "population explosion."

Many people are increasingly concerned about the growth of the world's population. Some have suggested that it represents a serious crisis. I'll spend some time on that topic in a future column. But let me tell you about a remarkable young woman and her mother who spoke at the Life Forum conference. The young woman, a pre-med student, is Sarah Smith. Her mother, a minister's wife, is Betty. Their presentation began with Betty's testimony. Seems that over twenty years ago Betty was the mother of a growing family of children. With the addition of another baby, Betty found more and more people willing to offer critical comment. Some, in fact, advised her that large families were creating a "population problem." Others told her that having too many children was a fundamentally irresponsible choice to make. Betty started to own their reasoning. She started to believe that she should limit any future plans for more children. And then it happened. Betty discovered that she was, in fact, pregnant again. Having embraced the reasoning that more children was a selfish choice, Betty determined that she would abort this latest pregnancy. Like millions before and since, she scheduled her appointment and with many misgivings went through with her abortion. The reality of what she'd done came crashing through when a nurse at the abortion facility asked a simple question. "Do you have any other children?"

In that moment, Betty knew precisely what had taken place. The nurse was asking about "other children" in recognition of the child who had just been terminated in that abortion clinic. Betty was immediately flooded with feelings of regret. In the traumatic months which followed, Betty prayed and cried and wished things had been different. One night, she discovered an answer to her prayers. While reading a book in bed, the book, which rested on her stomach, suddenly jumped. Betty says she blamed it on supper! But as the night wore on, the truth gradually became real. Someone was alive in her. Betty went to her doctor and obtained a pregnancy test. The results were positive. Betty, it seems, had been pregnant with twins. The abortionist had managed to eliminate one, a baby boy, but had been unaware that hiding in another corner of the womb was a beautiful girl who would be named Sarah.

Betty's doctor, however, was adamantly opposed to the continuance of the pregnancy. His reasoning was simple: If this child survived the trauma of an abortion, she would surely be born with deeply serious birth defects. It was, the doctor insisted, Betty's duty to terminate this pregnancy. Betty had another view. Having dealt for months with the pain and guilt of knowing that she'd made the mistake of aborting the child she named Andrew, she wasn't going to make a make a similar choice. This unborn child would live and be loved. In Betty's soul, Sarah was seen as another chance, as an opportunity to be reconciled. Sarah was born and is extraordinary. Her legs were impaired by the abortionist's instrument. She did require a number of surgeries to correct the damage but she is a bright, incredibly beautiful, talented and sensitive gift from God. And when Sarah got up to speak at the Life Forum conference, she acted as a human face for all the unborn children who never had the chance to be born.

Sarah's talk was awesome. She told us that the word "abortion" has really lost its meaning because it has become an abstraction. We talk more about the act of abortion instead of focusing on the person who dies in an abortion. Sarah challenged us to see that every child who dies in an abortion is a unique, individual, intended and precious life. Sarah reminded us that the choice for abortion cannot be separated from an awareness that someone is being put to death.

Sarah told us that for many years after her birth she felt something missing, she felt a loneliness in her life, she felt an absence. When she mentioned this to her counselor, he asked if he could mention this feeling to her mother Betty. On hearing this, Betty knew she had to tell Sarah the whole story. The missing presence she felt was the absence of her brother Andrew because, Sarah believes, even in the womb there was a bond between these children; and that bond had been permanently altered when one was taken from life and one remained.

Sarah Smith is a poignant and powerful reminder. She stands before us to tell us the truth about abortion. It's not just about rights. It's not just about choices. It's also about real people denied the fundamental right to "life, liberty and the pursuit of happiness." Sarah and her brave mother Betty want others to look abortion in the face. They want to remind America that God places before each of us the choice between life and death. Survivors Sarah and Betty Smith urge us: choose life!

Questions for Reflection

- In this story the truth set Betty and Sarah free. What past or present life choice has made you free?
- How has sharing this truth been lifegiving for others?

Death Penalty

PRO-DEATH penalty sentiment seems to be everywhere. Polls indicate that the vast majority of Americans want it. Media folks are telling us about the rising wave of violent crime, and we're responding by demanding that the culprits be "fried." So this might be a good time for us to examine why the American bishops have so steadfastly opposed the use of capital punishment.

The Church maintains that all life is a gift from God. And since God is the author of life, only God has the right to bring life to completion. When we as individuals, or we as the state, decide to terminate life, we take on a godly role which is simply not ours to take. And the fact that the criminal is "guilty" does not diminish his or her worth in the eyes of God. Christ came to love and cherish all, the good and the less good. That's the fundamental theological reason for opposing the death penalty. But there are also a number of practical considerations to ponder.

For instance, there is no convincing evidence that the death penalty will prevent crime or deter crime. In fact, just the opposite seems true. In a state like Florida, for example, the death penalty has been used with some frequency. That state's rate of violence continues to climb nonetheless. In a country like Canada, however, where the death penalty has been revoked, the incidence of violent crimes has diminished.

There is also the issue of fairness. People avoid the death penalty if they've got enough money to pay for convincing and effective attorneys. Black Americans are far more likely to die in the electric chair than white Americans. Ninety percent of those living on death row today have no money to hire a lawyer.

Another interesting aspect of the capital punishment issue is its use among the sexes. The death penalty seems to discriminate against men. Forty percent of the homicides committed in our nation are done by women, but only one percent of those living on death row are women. Since 1930 there have been 6,432 instances of capital punishment in our country. Of that number, only 56 women have been executed.

Then there's the issue of human error. Not everyone convicted by a jury is, in fact, guilty. When you sentence someone to life in prison, these errors can be corrected. But we can't correct our error once the prisoner has been terminated. How often, you might ask, do we actually execute the wrong person? Well, criminal justice experts suggest that one in twenty of those executed are, in fact, innocent. For these poor souls, capital punishment represents the unfixable mistake.

Then there's the issue of cost. It is not cheaper to execute a prisoner. Life imprisonment is one-half the cost. It costs, on an average, about $1.8 million for every execution we undertake in America. Each case also ties up the criminal justice system for at least a decade.

We can also note the company we keep as a pro-death penalty nation. Europe and Latin America do not have a death penalty. Great Britain and Canada have resisted the call to reinstate it. But Communist China, Russia and Iran use the death penalty widely. Is that the company we want to keep? Some will say it's a matter of justice. But I suspect our real motives have more to do with revenge. We're frustrated by the ugliness and the evil of violent crime. It revolts us and makes us want to right a vicious wrong. Justice should be done. But does killing the killer really bring us any peace of mind or soul?

Question for Reflection

- Beyond the practical reasons to oppose the death penalty is God's right to begin and end it. How does this truth affect your position on capital punishment?

Littleton, Colorado

ONLY days after the terrible shootings and everyone had an opinion. It's about handguns. It's about television and its violent messages. It's about the breakdown in parent-child communication. It's about cults and subcults. It's about increasing teenage isolation and alienation. All valid points of view, and all, I suspect, missing the essence. That essential factor was danced around on the highly rated Rosie O'Donnell show. Her guest was Congresswoman Carolyn McCarthy, speaking eloquently about her own tragic loss of her husband to unrestricted handguns. O'Donnell, who feels most things passionately, was in high gear on this tragedy. Her solution was simple: ban all guns. An understandable demand on the day after innocent teens were slaughtered by their pathetic executioners. Powerless teens feeling momentarily potent while armed with high powered manpower. The faces of the accused are striking in their ordinariness. They could be anyone's child.

But nowhere in this deeply felt television program did anyone venture near the always controversial and nonetheless vital issue of abortion and the culture which fosters it. At the most basic level, at our most vulnerable, at the point at which we are pure potential, our society permits and sometimes encourages the extermination of pre-born millions. Mrs. McCarthy, so impressive in arguing for the protection of children from handguns, fails to mention her own vote (three times!) for Partial Birth Abortion. And where's the difference? Partial Birth Abortion destroys a fully-formed and healthy nine month old about-to-be born baby. If it's not life worthy of protection then, when is life worthy of defense?

And what about Rosie O'Donnell? She identifies herself as pro-choice, strongly stands with and endorsed Bill Clinton and is the mother by adoption of two children she is said to adore. Again, doesn't she get the inconsistency? The children she adopted might, in the twinkling of an eye, have been snuffed out by the choice we call abortion. It was perfectly legal for the mothers who conceived Rosie's babies to have chosen the babies' death. Choice does that.

Both Carolyn McCarthy and Rosie O'Donnell aren't bad people, they just see selectively. They hate violence, grieve over the loss of some innocent children, but fail to see the connection. When a society blithely terminates over a million children a year it sows the seed for widespread disregard for life at every stage.

Do a search of media stories over the past year and see what I mean. You'll find several hundred pieces about the concern many in the Hollywood community have for animal rights. Pickets. Protests. Boycotts. All to stop the fur industry. Do a similar check on media folks speaking out on the greatest violence in our age, the abortion of our most precious resource: you'll find precious little. It's the rare voice. Patricia Heaton is one such voice. She plays Debra, a wife and mother on the successful sitcom "Everybody Loves Raymond." In a recent letter in support of Feminists for Life, Heaton wrote: "Doing the right thing is hard, especially in a world where everyone seems to underestimate women, a world that thinks children are expendable." And where does her concern for life originate? In her own life's journey: "In deciding to take on this challenge of being publicly pro-life, I looked back to my own roots. My mother and I had a relatively short time together. She died when I was twelve years old, but she instilled in me a deep respect for life, for women and for the truth." Heaton's onto the truth, I think. And how refreshing it is to see a very public person willing to stand the tide of those who find defending animal rights a more sympathetic cause than human rights.

On "Personally Speaking," the show I host on behalf of the Catholic Communications Campaign, I recently interviewed actress Margaret Colin. She's a star of movies ("Independence

Day"), television ("Chicago Hope") and the Broadway stage ("Jackie"). She's also an unrepentant pro-lifer who told us that nothing, not the money, success or adulation she receives can hold a candle to the value of her two young sons. And in her testimony is the meaning of our culture's deepest hope. We cannot be surprised or shocked when innocent teenagers are slaughtered within a culture which says it's okay to legally kill a defenseless unborn child. Pre-born children and sixteen year old teenagers are equally human, have equal right to be here, and have an equal right to be rescued from purposeless violence. We will continue to mourn our dead until we stop all the violence, beginning in the womb of life.

Questions for Reflection

● Which for you is the most convincing reason to oppose abortion?

● What makes it difficult for you to say no to abortion?

Priesthood and Politics

A secular newspaper featured a piece recently on a race for the United States House of Representatives. In that article on possible candidates for Congressional office was yours truly.

In fact, I had discussed a possible candidacy with several party and elected officials. And the temptation to make a go of it was very real. After all, we live in a country chock full of laws, some good and some less so. Those laws are made at several levels, among them the Congress. And what a bully pulpit it could be in promoting ideals which every priest treasures.

The reaction among people to the article was of two kinds. Younger folks thought the idea of a priest in elective office unusual. Folks who've been around were less nonplused, they've seen it happen before. At a number of local or municipal levels, priests have held office in the past. And for almost a decade a Massachusetts district was represented in Congress by Jesuit Father Robert Drinan. So it's certainly not a new concept.

Then in 1980, after serious consideration, the Holy See issued a set of directives which effectively banned priests from holding office. There was and continues to be lots of speculation about why Pope John Paul II, no slouch when it comes to the workings of politics, would ban other clerics from direct involvement. My own idea? I think the Holy Father had two concerns, one theoretical and one practical.

The practical implications were determined by the priests who were, at that time, holding office. In some cases they were clearly not reflecting the mind of Paul II. Two examples suffice.

Father Drinan is a top scholar and law school professor. He's also written and spoken, with great eloquence about the needs of the poor. So from this viewpoint, he and Rome are in perfect unity. But his thought also supports the right of society to choose the abortion of pre-born children.

In fact, while in Congress, Father Drinan had an almost flawless pro-choice voting record This included not only support for the fundamental right to choose abortion, but laws which would have expanded and promoted that right. In short, he was a priest who helped make abortion an even more deeply ingrained part of our society. In his defense, he'd probably say that he was "personally opposed" to abortion, but felt that people of every economic strata should have an equal right to abortion, even if that meant using taxpayer funding for abortion in order to achieve equal availability.

The full wisdom of Pope John Paul II's decision to instruct Father Drinan's resignation came more fully to light several years ago. In his public pronouncements (especially in a piece published in The New York Times), Father Drinan spoke out in favor of Bill Clinton's support for partial-birth abortion. And although he has since renounced his support, Father Drinan's earlier endorsement of this inhuman procedure would seem to lend weight to Rome's restrictions on priests in politics.

At the same time, another priest also held government office. His name was Father Ernesto Cardenal, and he served as the Minister of Culture in Nicaragua. Problem there: his government was led by a Marxist political party, the Sandinistas. Pope John Paul, who probably understood more about Communist/Marxist oppression than most churchmen, was understandably troubled by Father Cardenal's role in the Ortega administration.

In both the Drinan and Cardenal cases, the Holy See instructed them to cease and desist from their political roles. Father Drinan, to his credit, obeyed. Father Cardenal continued in office, fomenting a public chastisement by John Paul II during his pastoral visit to Nicaragua.

In these cases we witnessed the fundamental difficulty with priests in politics or elective office. On one hand, office could be a wonderful opportunity to promote Gospel values. But on the other, it can easily lead to positions which compromise Gospel teachings. And politics, being of its nature a place where compromise is standard fare, offers a difficult breeding ground for consistent fidelity to Church teaching.

So what, then, is our proper role toward government? Well, we clearly have a role. And it involves the right and obligation to be advocates, to be spokespersons, and to challenge laws we see as unjust, supporting and proposing laws which improve society. We just can't hold office.

Some priests, probably reacting to the limits placed on priests like Drinan and Cardenal, have avoided a role in the public debates of politics and government. But stepping out of the arena serves no one. We belong in the public square encouraging, teaching, admonishing, and being a voice for the voiceless. Anything less constitutes the sin of omission.

Questions for Reflection

- Do you think that the refusal of the Vatican to allow priests to hold public office is curtailing their ability to promote Gospel values in the marketplace?
- How can you share the Gospel mandate of justice for the oppressed?

Part III

Celebrities and Heroes

Speaking of Faith

PERSONALLY Speaking is a television program of the Catholic Communications Campaign. Produced by the United States Catholic Conference, this half-hour interview show attempts to give people in government, in the hierarchy, in the arts and public people of varied backgrounds and interests a chance to articulate something they rarely get asked about: their personal faith. It's a fascinating irony of modern times that as television and radio now, more than ever, attempt to investigate the deepest parts of personal behavior, we still rarely ask people what makes them tick spiritually. There are so many stories waiting to be told!

As the host of this program, it's my job to ask the pertinent questions. Questions about faith, ideals, motivations, life goals, and the disappointments which often populate our life journeys.

Recently, we taped a number of shows with people from the Hollywood community. Their forthrightness was staggering. Not only because they were people of faith, but also because they were refreshed and delighted to be asked about their personal relationships with God.

Our guests included actor Carroll O'Connor, known now and forever for his starring role in television's "All in the Family," and "In the Heat of the Night." A lifelong Catholic who practices his faith, Mr. O'Connor talked about the pain of maintaining hope in the face of despair. His personal cross, shared lovingly with his wife Nancy, was the loss of his only child. His son, Hugh, after years of struggle, lost his battle with cocaine, addiction and suicide. Trust in the Lord was and is a saving grace for this heart-broken father.

Another guest was the luminous actress and singer Ann Jillian. Blessed with talent, beauty and a winning personality, Ms. Jillian shared with us her battles with breast cancer, her longing for a child for over 15 years of marriage, and the miracle of her son's birth. Her mastectomy, intensive chemothera-py, and the reality of being in her 40s, led many to encourage Ms. Jillian to terminate her long-awaited child. Her trust in God's plan led Ann and husband Andy to say yes to the unknown. That choice led her to the boundless joy she knows today as the mother of a son she adores.

Jack and Pat Shea were also our guests. Jack is the president of the Director's Guild of America, his wife Pat a very success-ful screenwriter. Both shared the vital importance of faith in their lives and work. Pat spoke of her determination to raise her six children first, returning to school and a career after that, and the grace she finds in bringing her Catholic ideals into the world of television. Together with Jack, and at the invitation of Cardinal Roger Mahony, Pat wrote a screenplay for a video called "The Right Choice." It addresses wonderfully the issue of abortion by giving the pre-born child a voice. Told that working on such a politically incorrect project would be hurt-ful to their careers, Pat and Jack persisted. Faith and family have always been central in the lives of these committed Catholic Christians.

Stacy Keach, star of the Fox series "Titus" was boldly forth-coming in sharing his journey of faith. It included his recollec-tion of days battling addiction, and time spent in jail when his life spun out of control. Now married to a Polish Catholic actress, Mr. Keach attends Our Lady of Malibu Church regu-larly. He did this first to please his wife and assist his children in their faith development. But recently, the Protestant-raised Mr. Keach has found new serenity in his adopted home. He's now in the process of converting to Roman Catholicism.

Tom Bosley was my guest. Mr. Cunningham of "Happy Days" and the character who starred in "The Father Dowling Mysteries," is as kind and gentle and sweet in person as you'd guess from his television persona. Raised in the Jewish faith, he is a man of deep conviction. Married to a Catholic woman after the untimely sickness and death of his first wife, Mr. Bosley has expressed a deep affection for the Catholic Church.

Other great guests included comedian Steve Allen, actor Johnathan Schaech, Jim Hawkins (a star of the film "It's a Wonderful Life"), Warner Brothers Music President Phil Quartararo, producer-director Father Ellwood Kaiser, screenwriter Barbara Nicolosi, producer David Schall, Catholics In Media spiritual moderator, Father Ken Deasy and actress Catherine Hicks (star of television's impressive "Seventh Heaven" program).

Every guest celebrated the opportunity to talk publicly about their faith, something they almost never get asked about. Young actor Johnathan Schaech (star of Tom Hanks' movie "That Thing You Do," and television's "Houdini" special) said with exasperation: "Interviewers ask you what color you like best, what clothes you like to wear, what kind of person you want to date, what you eat for breakfast? They never ask these kinds of questions, like what do you believe in? What does your faith mean to you? Who is God in your daily life? These are questions that ultimately matter the most."

Thanks to the American bishops for letting a program like "Personally Speaking" happen.

Questions for Reflection

- Why do questions like "What does your faith mean to you?" and "Who is God in your daily life?" matter the most?

- Why are people reluctant to ask or to share these questions?

Maxwell's Values

THE March, 1982, issue of New York magazine headlined him as "The Next Overnight Sensation." And, indeed, that's what he was for a while. The English actor Maxwell Caulfield arrived in New York to rave reviews. Caulfield starred in the stage production of "Entertaining Mr. Sloan." He became the talk of the town, admired for his acting, his looks, and his style. He was seen as the next big "star." Compared to another megawatt performer, John Travolta, Maxwell was selected by producer Allan Carr to take the lead in the promising movie musical "Grease 2." Co-starring Michelle Pfeiffer, the film would cement Caulfield's already expanding reputation.

Around the same time, Maxwell took himself a stellar wife. The actress Juliet Mills, known to most Americans as Nanny on the hit television series "Nanny and the Professor," became his bride; and the two burned up the gossip pages. Not only were they a striking acting couple, but the new Mrs. Caulfield was significantly older than the 21-year-old actor. Tabloids had a field day about this unlikely coupling. And then the other shoe dropped. Maxwell's expected success never happened. "Grease 2" opened to terrible reviews. The promise of a huge financial windfall never occurred. The overnight sensation took a nose dive. Oh, there were comebacks along the journey, but they were hard won. Probably his best known exposure was as Miles Colby, the spoiled son of Charlton Heston on the television series "The Colbys" (a spin-off of Dynasty). He toured without much fanfare in plays like "Loot!" and "The Elephant Man." He earned very respectable reviews in a film called "The Boys Next Door," a drama co-starring Charlie Sheen. But, by and large, the dramatic stardom never happened.

When I interviewed Mr Caulfield, he gave me the chance to ask a question I've always wondered about. What do you do when the promises, the expectations don't happen? Or how do you continue to remain upbeat and positive when life doesn't go as you'd planned? His answers were refreshing and a valuable lesson for any young person with a dream and the possibility of disappointment.

Caulfield said that he was able to face the let-down because he had the support of a true love, his wife. Caulfield was able to see beyond the superficial judgments of age or looks. He recognized that his wife was a person of strength, insight, loyalty and goodness. And in choosing love for the right reasons, he benefitted richly in tough times. He'd married someone who really believed in being there through the good and less good times of life.

Maxwell also shared that he started to realize that being evaluated on the basis of his looks was a set-up for failure. All looks fade; and if we don't develop the interior person underneath, we'll never find life-long happiness or fulfillment. The actor also spoke of his developing recognition that, in the end, we're all called to admit our dependence on God. Truth is, we're all connected to the source of life; and we only find peace when we're conforming to His will.

Maxwell Caulfield may not be Tom Hanks. He may not enjoy huge success. But he does know who he is. Through the bumps and disappointments of life, he's come to recognize what really matters: true and committed love, a sense of worth based on the interior person and an honest reliance on God as the source of all we are or hope to be.

Question for Reflection

● How do you continue to remain upbeat and positive when life doesn't go as you'd planned?

Phoebe's Faith

L IKE most film buffs, I first noticed Ruth Warrick when she played opposite Orson Welles in the classic "Citizen Kane." As the wife he betrays, Ruth Warrick was by turns light and breezy, dark and angry. She was also radiantly beautiful. Many films, and several televisions series later (including "Peyton Place" and "As the World Turns"), Ruth continues to act in the long-playing soap opera "All my Children." As a character known as Phoebe Tyler Wallingford, Ms. Warrick has grown and evolved as a character we once hated and now view with benign appreciation. Twenty-seven years of familiarity will do that!

Through our mutual friend, the suave and charming actor Douglas Fairbanks Jr., I had the chance to meet and talk with Ruth Warrick. At 80 she is still lovely to look at and delightful at the art of conversation. Our visit led to a series of interviews on my Telecare program, "Let's Talk." Ms. Warrick told many Hollywood-style stories and entranced us with her energy and her incredible memory. But of all her stories, it was a challenge to her faith which struck me as her most arresting tale because in it, Ruth faced a compromise we all encounter.

Raised as a Baptist in St. Joseph, Missouri, Ruth Warrick was trained by her family and her community to prize and treasure her Christian faith. She knows the Bible chapter and verse. Through the good and bad times of life, this dedication to the Lord has sustained her. When she came to New York three decades ago, Ms. Warrick sought out a variety of churches looking for a place where she could be spiritually fed. She ultimately landed in the Unity Church and obtained a license and certification as a metaphysics teacher from the School of Practical Christianity.

On one particular occasion, the members of her Church were celebrating her latest accomplishments. Ruth was asked to give a talk to the very ecumenical group gathered at her

Church. During her remarks, Ruth Warrick was decidedly strong in giving credit for her life, her talents and her gifts to Jesus Christ. She told the assembled guests that her personal relationship with Jesus Christ was the center of her life. And she explained that without Christ in her life, she would have no mooring, no center, no ability to place the vicissitudes of life in perspective. Politely received following her speech, Ruth Warrick was pretty well snubbed by the fellow who acted as director or guru of the gathering. Clearly her remarks had not pleased him. Disturbed by his reaction, Ms. Warrick sought him out to ask why he had responded so coldly to her speech.

The director explained that their Church was a fairly mixed group, that people of various faiths and outlooks would always be present. It was, he suggested, inappropriate to focus such direct attention on the person of Jesus Christ. A more broad-based talk about God, a more watered-down version of some amorphous "higher power" would be preferable. The Church director suggested that in the future, Ruth should refrain from any specific reference to Jesus Christ.

For Ruth Warrick, this was simply unacceptable. It would, she reasoned, be like saying we loved mothers in general instead of naming the specific person who parented us. God does not exist for Ruth Warrick in "general terms." He is a specific and personal friend. He is the person we call Jesus Christ, the redeemer, the messiah, the Lord.

Throughout our society, we're often asked to water down or compromise our particular beliefs. We're asked to treat all religions as though there were no differences. And while it's surely true that we're obligated to offer every religious perspective the honor and reverence it warrants, we're also commanded by our personal integrity to be true to a personal vision of the Lord. He reveals Himself to us in specific and intimate ways. We shouldn't compromise our truth just so that we can "fit it" to some homogenized vision of the deity.

Ruth Warrick is one bright, classy and impressive person. But, for me, none of her acting accomplishments can match the personal dedication and witness she gives on behalf of Jesus Christ. He's her Lord, and He's non-negotiable. By the way, she still calls Him by name!

Questions for Reflection

- Whether it's actresses like Phoebe, or the latest sports champion or rock phenomenon, Jesus Christ is being name dropped by the high achievers. Does this give you the go ahead you need?

- How do you overcome the urge to compromise your beliefs?

Margot's Choices

IF you read People magazine, you might remember actress Margot Kidder on the front cover. The article recounted her nervous breakdown, her career-driven life, the ups and downs of the Hollywood lifestyle, and the effects an assortment of lovers had on her emotional stability. Details were given of her suicide attempts, multiple failed marriages, and the fragile and troubled relationship she's had with her only child, a daughter named Maggie. It's a sad article in that it took a public breakdown and the experience of living among the homeless in a cardboard shelter for Margot Kidder to arrive on the cover of the nation's leading personality magazine. I'm sure that Ms. Kidder would have preferred to be featured there because of her successful career, not because of her destructive personal life.

The article identified her as a manic-depressive personality and proceeds to tell us that over two million Americans suffer from this emotional instability, a condition which causes the sufferer to experience incredible highs and equally disorienting lows.

As I read the eight-page article, I kept waiting for our friends in the news media to tell the whole story. Not surprisingly, the details I sought never appeared in print. It's not politically correct to highlight a dimension of Margot Kidder's life experience which probably helped to set her on this downward spiral. Drug and alcohol abuse gets mentioned, career highs and lows get mentioned, financial insecurities are made clear, but nowhere do we hear about a fundamental decision Kidder made early in life, or of its lifelong consequences.

At the age of 16 Margot Kidder began a rebellion against her parents and all authority. She fled her home and sought out the high life in Toronto. She took a lover who was old enough to be her father. At the age of 18, she became pregnant by this considerably older man. And although he was happy for the pregnancy and wished to have the child, he nonetheless supported

Margot Kidder's wish to abort the baby. Ms. Kidder admits that her career ambitions fueled the decision to terminate her pregnancy. In a book entitled *The Choices We Made,* she writes: "I knew that having a baby would mean the end of everything I'd wanted since I was nine. I have diaries from back then saying `I'm going to Hollywood and be a movie star.' I was ambitious and determined. I wasn't emotionally mature enough to see that a baby would add to my life. I wasn't capable of that kind of love at that age."

Following her abortion, Ms. Kidder came to recognize the consequences of her choices. She tells us: "I remember beginning to weep because it seemed to me that I had done a terrible, terrible thing. I wept for what would have been my baby, and I remember saying `I want my baby back.' I wept and wept and wept. Subsequently the nightmares began, the most horrible, horrible nightmares. They were constant and went on for a long time." And then Ms. Kidder revealingly admits that "the nightmares stopped when I had my child Maggie, which was when I was 27 years old."

From 18 until 27 Margot Kidder experienced severe emotional trauma which was directly related to the painful choice and frightening consequences of abortion. Most of the decisions we make have an effect. There are always consequences, some positive, others negative. In making moral decisions, we always need to examine what the effect will be. We don't live in a vacuum, and consequences flow out of the choices we make. I'm sorry that in telling the Margot Kidder story, People magazine decided to share only part of the truth.

When a friend has sex, gets pregnant and considers the choice of abortion, a true friend doesn't bury or deny the consequences which may result. A real friend tells the truth, that there is no such thing as actions without consequences. Margot Kidder's life is a warning alarm. Let's learn from her and her challenging life journey.

In her role as Lois Lane in the Superman movies, Ms. Kidder is always protected by her mythical boyfriend. In real life, actress Margot Kidder was far more vulnerable. The only true protection we have are the right choices and the friends who help us make them.

Questions for Reflection

- Aelred of Rievaulx, a 12th century monk, is best known for his treatise on friendship "the perfect gift of nature and grace." Make a list of what you consider true marks of a genuine friendship.
- Make a list of the friends who hit the mark?

Dare to Dream

FEW people don't long for success. It's a natural human desire. It's a concept usually connected to thoughts of money, position, respectability and popularity. But successful people often claim that the road to success is much tougher than we might expect. One of the best books published on the topic is aimed at young people. It's called *Dare to Dream*, and it's written by Olympic Gold Medalist Tim Daggett. On July 31, 1984, in Los Angeles, Daggett stunned America and the world with his perfect "10" on the gymnastics high bar. He became an instant American hero and made it possible for the whole American team to cop the gold Olympic medal.

This is a sport long dominated by other nations. I highlight Tim Daggett's book, however, because in it he takes the concept of success and dissects it. He takes us painful step by painful step through the arduous and rewarding process. Here are some of the ideas he heralds:

(1) You don't have to be the most talented person in your field to succeed. It certainly helps to be naturally gifted, but a person can often compensate for the lack of natural talent by adding in strong measures of devotion, concentration and self-esteem. Says Tim Daggett, "It isn't necessarily the 'naturally gifted' people who make it but rather the ones who have a dream and are willing to pay the price to make that dream come true."

(2) Coupled with that dream is the willingness to take whatever talent you've got and form it by tireless effort. In his lengthy chapter entitled "The Dream" Tim writes of the unromantic, the boring and the repetitive days he spent honing his gymnastic skills. And, he reminds us, this work had to be done with no assurance that the golden prize would actually ever happen. In other words he says success is impossible without faith. Tim Daggett had enormous amounts of trust, in himself, in the future and in the power of determination.

(3) Daggett writes a lot about his family. He's one of seven children. And apparently he was, from birth, different from the rest in looks, in temperament and in personality. But from an early age his mother, in particular, communicated to him the idea that "being different" isn't necessarily a bad thing. In fact, his parents seemed to believe that following the unique traits of our individual personality is a blessing. That celebration of Tim's uniqueness helped him to move forward, unencumbered by the differences in his goals or dreams.

(4) Much is written today about children who are "hyperactive." In fact, there are an assortment of drugs which are prescribed for young people to control this hyperactivity. Reflecting on his childhood, Daggett suggests that he probably was one such child. His energy levels knew no bounds, he was often "out of control," and limiting him became a full-time job for his overtaxed parents. Daggett thanks his parents for working through his childhood overdrive without resorting to drugs. He believes that their patience and understanding helped to re-direct that hyperactivity in a positive way.

(5) More telling than Tim Daggett's chapter on getting prepared for competition, or even the parts where he writes about the glory days of the Olympics, are his reflections about life "Beyond the Dream." It is a sensitive and solid testament to the importance of knowing what really matters. Because in the face of overwhelming media attention and public adulation, Daggett ultimately remembered that his family, his long-time friends and his sense of himself were far more real, far more important than the fleeting spotlight. Tim reminds anyone who has a dream to enjoy the perks but to remain rooted in things and people who last.

(6) In the final chapter of his book, appropriately called "The Nightmare," Daggett shows us the greatness of a real Olympian. Following his astonishing success at the 1984 Olympics, the world seemed unlimited. But in 1987, in practic-

ing for his next competition, Daggett fell 15 feet to the ground. He ruptured a disc and did significant damage to his nerves. Against all expectations, Daggett persisted in getting better and competing in the World Championships at Rotterdam. In that competition Daggett faced his greatest personal crisis. He sustained an injury to his leg so serious, some doctors considered the need for amputation. In this amazing profile in courage and hope, Tim Daggett shows us the importance of dedication and persistence. Daggett once again became a world-class competitor.

Tim Daggett is now retired from active competition. With great poignancy, he recounts the day of his final attempts at making the Olympic trials. And even in his failure, he demonstrates great class. In his loss, another young man has the potential to realize "the dream." Tim delights in people obtaining their dreams. He now coaches kids in his native West Springfield, Massachusetts. He also gives motivational talks to people around the country. His message is important not only because it highlights the potency of dreams, determination and courage but because Daggett never fails to celebrate what we're really here for. In the closing chapter of *Dare to Dream*, Tim Daggett says, "Well, I guess the glory days are behind me now. But beneath it all, I know I have what's really important: the love of my family, the knowledge that I have succeeded, and the experience to know that if I give it everything I've got, I can make the dreams for the rest of my life come true."

Question for Reflection

- Tim Daggett's victorious comeback after his injury is proof that " In a dark time, the eye begins to see." Share your personal experience of God's faithfulness in helping you to realize your dreams.

One Life at a Time

SOMETIMES people with enormous success and wealth can become incredibly detached from life. Not so Wellington Mara. The co-owner of the New York Giants is very connected to real people and real life. He realizes that it's never enough to be against something (like abortion), unless you're also committed to being for something (namely, helping a mother and her child to make it). So Mara has dedicated himself to an organization called Pro-Life Athletes. This growing body is filled with men and women who play professional sports. Different as these athletes are, they share one common bond. Each believes that abortion should be the choice no one has to make. Toward that end, the athletes travel our nation to speak on behalf of homes for unwed mothers, and for crisis pregnancy centers. Their support has been an extraordinary blessing for these maternity centers. At one dinner I coordinated to help maternity homes, the football players Mark Bavaro (then of the Giants) and Mark Boyer (then of the Jets) came and spoke to those present. The night produced over $60,000 for the mothers and their children.

These maternity homes or crisis pregnancy centers offer true and loving alternatives to abortion. For many teen-age and young adult mothers-to-be, pregnancy is a frightening and unsupported reality. Family members and friends encourage many to abort. The young mother is told that if she has her baby, she'll have to drop out of school and go on public assistance. In the face of these fearful predictions, maternity homes offer a gentle assurance there is no need to fear, that life can go on successfully with a baby. Some maternity homes offer shelter and support through the period of pregnancy. Others offer a place to live and grow for a year or two after the baby's delivery. Those who live at the homes continue their educations and also develop career prospects. In fact, studies indicate that for many of those who live in maternity homes, they are even more focused and more directed in their lives because of the experience of childbirth.

One of these remarkable homes is Mother of Good Counsel House in Roosevelt, New York. Run by Oblate Sisters, this maternity home has given many mothers and their babies a new lease on life. It's ironic that Sisters who staff the home are primarily from Colombia, South America. There was a time when our country sent missionaries around the world to assist the peoples of other lands. Today, they come to us in an effort to help us re-embrace values like the protection of innocent life.

At a recent dinner to assist the Oblate Sisters' home, Mr. Mara sent one of his players to speak. His name is Carlton Bailey, and he was starting lineman for the Giants. He came to us after a grueling day of practice, and after the dinner would be returning to Giants Stadium for more physical therapy. In talking to Mr. Bailey before the dinner, I asked him what motivated his interest in teen-age mothers and their babies. His answer put a human face on why pro-lifers do what they do: Carlton told me that his own mother had been sexually active in her early teen years. In fact, she was pregnant with him when she was 15. Many would have encouraged her to abort. But the courage she had to give life meant that Carlton Bailey could be with us to help others just like his Mom. Mr. Bailey deeply loves his mother. His presence that night was an attempt to make it possible for other young women, like his Mom, to be supported in their personal choices for life. Maternity homes mean that Carlton Baileys as yet unborn will have a chance to live.

Question for Reflection

- Wellington Mara and Carlton Bailey speak out against abortion and give women the opportunity to keep their children and their dreams. How does their example help you to be a defender of the unborn?

Chris Farley, R.I.P.

SHORTLY before Christmas 1997, the entertainment world lost actor/comedian Chris Farley at the age of 33. The cause is still unclear, but few doubt that the combination of food, drugs, alcohol and an out-of-control lifestyle collectively combined to do in this gifted funnyman. Looking for a meaning behind futile loss is oftentimes a difficult task, but in Farley's case there are some necessary issues which need to be confronted. First, our national delight in making fun of overweight people has to end. It's a quick and sure destroyer of self-image. Compulsive overeating is a disorder, not a cause for delight or laughter. And mocking the illness is a particularly self-defeating practice when studies indicate that a majority of Americans are presently overweight.

The popular media also has a responsibility in the demise of people like Chris Farley because they both create and then destroy fragile souls like his by the temptation of easy and outrageous income without regard to the devastating effects such money will cause to those unable to manage their "success." Chris Farley was apparently someone who could not handle the sudden and ready access to million-dollar temptations, but the payers were unconcerned about the payee's proclivities. They wanted a popular product, and consequences be damned. Chris Farley's life is also a morality tale about the heroes we choose and where those choices may lead us. In interview after interview, Farley recounted how taken he'd been as a youngster with the success of another actor/comedian, John Belushi; and in seriously parallel ways, they shadowed each other. Like Farley, Belushi was surrounded by "friends" or sycophants who fed him the means for self-destruction; and like Belushi, Farley had to pay too dear a price for his relatively few moments of fame and fortune. It's hard to draw good from a bad model; and in Belushi, Chris Farley had an equally tragic and misguided twin. You'll note that I put the word friends in quotation marks above because Chris Farley's death reminds us that folks will all too often term themselves as close friends to a guy like Farley. Yet their collaborative activities are the direct opposite of something a friend would or should do. True friends don't sit and watch their friend get blindly drunk. True friends don't participate in drugfests or help to supply a deadly habit. True friends don't procure sexual favors for a poor man who really needed a loyal and loving girlfriend. And true friends don't view other friends as an unlimited bank account for easy dipping. Yet that's exactly the kind of "friends" Chris Farley had in abundance. They were takers, not people of caring; and they share in his untimely death. They were "friends" who aren't.

News reports indicate that Chris Farley, recognizing that he was mounted on a speeding train to nowhere, sought help in the 11th hour of his life. Just weeks before his death Chris asked a priest he knew to say a private Mass for an end to his destructive compulsions, but the healing was short-lived. There were just too many experiences of self-abuse, and Chris Farley was too far along the path of self-destruction. Everyone now admits that he was a kind, sweet, gentle and giving person. Everyone now tells us that he was gifted and filled with a tremendous promise. Everyone now says it's a tragedy, a shame, a great loss. But there are other Chris Farleys waiting to happen, other losses which can be avoided. Let's hope his death can teach us something about charity, about our misguided humor, about the responsibility that comes with money, and about the true meaning of friendship—lessons which might well have saved this good and needful man.

Question for Reflection

● Chris Farley's unfortunate life choices drive home the importance of surrounding yourself with nurturing people and avoiding "friends who aren't." Are there some changes you need to make in your choices?

The New Virgins

IF you've been watching much television in recent years, or attending many movies, you know that many teen features focus on the subject of losing your virginity. In years past it was pretty clearly understood that a person should treasure the gift of sexuality and share it only with a spouse. That's also been the consistent teaching of the Catholic Church. But sometime in the last few decades, Hollywood and much of the secular print media decided that virginity was passe, that experimentation was the desired norm.

It's amazing then to note a change in attitude coming from a number of impressive teens and young adults who believe differently from our media friends. A few outstanding examples come to mind. Enrique Iglesias is the leading Spanish language singing artist in the world. Yes, even a bigger seller than Ricky Martin! Listen to what he says about sharing his sexuality: "I am a virgin, but when you talk about it, please don't make fun. My future plan would be to get married and lose my virginity." Interesting, isn't it, that Enrique feels the need to ask that he not be mocked for deciding not to share the rich gift of human sexual love with someone until he gets married.

Then there's tennis star Anna Kournikova, a knockout Russian, who says without apology: "I'm still a virgin. I do not let anyone even have a peep in my bed . . . not for love or affection." Anna is matched in the strength of her convictions by actress LeeLee Sobieski. You may remember her as the star of the CBS miniseries "Joan of Arc." LeeLee has said, without equivocation; "I'm the first virgin playing Joan of Arc. I'm happy that's the way I am."

Up and coming movie and television star Jonathan Jackson has a similar view. You'll remember Jonathan as a regular on "General Hospital," and the movie "Deep End of the Ocean." Jackson suggests that his virginity is a natural extension of his religious faith and believes: "I'm a virgin because I put God before self. The sexy stuff of show business really contradicts what I believe."

Maybe the most potent statement about virginity came from L.A. Lakers' basketball star, A.C. Green. At age 36, Green confessed: "I'm still a virgin. I compare it to steak or hamburger. I expect the best for me, so as tempting as the hamburger may look, I know there's something better for me if I wait." A.C. goes on to explain: "I promised God this, and I'm not going to break it. I love myself and my future wife too much to just waste it. I look at it as a gift for one heckuva woman."

And for those who argue that maintaining virginity is a near-impossible task, Green says: "It's not hard. It's a commitment. I just tell them up front, right away. 'Look, I really want to get to know you better, but I'm not interested in going to bed with you.' " Clear talk, he suggests, is the best way to eliminate sexual pressure. It also clears the decks of role-playing and allows him to be true friends with the women he dates.

Green admits that like many high school boys, he used to lie about his success at sexual scoring. "I was the biggest liar there was. I told everybody whom I did it with, when, and how many times. All lies. I mean, don't get me wrong. I wanted to do it. I just never did. I think, looking back on it, God was protecting me." A.C. Green has gone a step further than just talking about the value of a chaste life, he's helping other young people to do the same. He's set up the A.C. Green Foundation to develop a curriculum for grades 6 through 12. Its aim is to give young persons the self-awareness, the self-esteem and the courage in the face of peer pressure to wait and treasure rightly the magnificent God-given gift of our sexual selves.

Questions for Reflection

- Are you surprised at these "true confessions"? Why?
- Next time someone tells you "nobody waits anymore" what will your answer be?

Giving Something Back

WHEN Churches around the country speak on the topic of stewardship, the discussion focuses on an appreciation for the ways in which we've been blessed by God, and encourages us, in turn, to share our gifts and blessings with others. For many, this involves a decision to become more deeply immersed in parish ministry. At one point in our parish, consideration of stewardship meant that several hundred people came forward to volunteer in helping others, or in simply becoming more active participants in parish life. For others, a commitment to stewardship involves taking stock of their unique talents or abilities and dedicating at least part of their time to sharing these with others. So, I know lawyers in the parish who offer pro-bono ("for the good," that is, without charge) assistance to those who might not otherwise afford legal counsel. So too, electricians, architects, plumbers and painters have all stepped forward to see that their gifts and talents and abilities can be used to keep the parish running smoothly.

Many more parishioners consider stewardship from a fiscal point of view, and make a deeper commitment of their financial "treasure" toward the parish. In many instances, people look at the financial blessings they've accrued and decide to more fully share those blessings with their worship community. In our parish, like so many others, stewardship has meant a significant increase in weekly collections as people take more seriously the spiritual obligation to give back to God and His people for the blessings received. That additional financial help makes it possible for the parish to grow in many ways, not least in its ability to assist the most needy. So sharing Time, Talent and Treasure are surely the ways many are responding to the call of stewardship.

Recently, I've become aware of yet another dimension of this spiritual generosity. And it involves using one's workplace as a means to serve others. In particular, I'm thinking of a man named Scotty Passarelli. Born in America but raised in Scotland, this Italian-Scottish-American hybrid has owned and operated a number of successful restaurants in the New York metropolitan area. His sons Ronny and Lenny have continued that tradition, and currently manage Bobby Van's Steakhouse in New York City. Scotty, a strong and colorful 72-year-old runs a restaurant called The New Yorker in Rockville Centre.

Like many food industry folks, he benefits from the strong economy and has a long-coming and incredibly loyal clientele. His food is very good, his staff like a family, but the real magnet is clearly this accented and energetic restaurateur. He's opinionated and tough, strong-willed and just slightly over-the-top in personality. All of which works to mask a heart of amazing generosity. Scotty is well aware of where he's headed. He harbors no illusions about living forever. Loving his wife Nina, his children and grandchildren immensely, he nonetheless realizes something vital: we're all going to die and we're all only able to take with us the good that we do on earth. Otherwise, before God, we stand naked. So Scotty's stewardship, not a recent development by the way, involves offering his workplace for charitable dinners. Not once in a while, mind you, but very often. And the charities are as varied as the human condition. I've witnessed dinners for homeless men and women, those who are hearing-impaired, those who are drug- or alcohol-addicted, women caught in a crisis pregnancy, those raising money to promote vocations to the priesthood and religious life and for women and their children who are physically, sexually or emotionally abused. And he's able to say that these charitable causes can look not to thousands, but hundreds of thousands of dollars raised to aid their needs.

This is just one man's way of making a difference, one person's attempt to give back for the good he's received. The New Yorker is still a business and Scotty is still very much an entrepreneur. Six nights a week, he's packing the place with regular customers. But one night a week he remembers those who lack for the basics of human decency. And his dinners literally save lives. Most everyone reading this column works, or has family in one business or another. And, yes, business is dedicated to making money and earning a living. But can you imagine how deeply we could transform our needful society if every business were dedicated to becoming a little more like Scotty Passarelli's New Yorker Restaurant—a place that takes in a goodly amount but remembers to give back as well. What a wave of good we could bring to bear if every employer started staff meetings this way: "Well, we've had a good week, and we've made a very decent profit. Now what can we give to those who have less?" Multiply that notion a thousand times and you've got a lot of healing help, you've got stewardship not only where we live and pray, but stewardship where we work each day.

How can your workplace become more like The New Yorker, a place of business success, but a place that never forgets the poor, the needful and those who count on us to care? Stewardship is about Time, Treasure and Talent. But it's also about making the place we work a source of generosity and mercy. Thanks, Scotty, for showing us how.

Question for Reflection

- Almost every company wants to improve their public image. How can you use Scotty's story to challenge your company to become a source of generosity and mercy?

Between the Lines

BOB Halligan, Jr. and Buddy Connolly are two outstanding musicians. They were my guests on "Personally Speaking" to discuss a new album by their group. The band's name and album's title are the same Ceili Rain (Ceili is pronounced "KAY-lee"). Ceili Rain is especially popular in country and Irish music circles.

Before interviewing Bob and Buddy, I listened to their new album. The songs were beautifully written and performed, and at first I chalked them up as being simply outstanding love songs. It wasn't until someone alerted me to the deeply religious faith of these guys that I decided to listen again. And sure enough, I had missed much of the import of Ceili Rain's message. These songs are love songs, but they're love songs with a difference. They speak about the incredible, unconditional, unlimited and freely given passion God has for His creation.

After years of popular success, writing for some of the biggest names in American pop music, Bob Halligan, Jr. decided there must be something more to life than pumping out hit records. He wanted his music to remain popular, but also to show people the love of God in songs which move us to recognize the awesome embrace of the Lord's constant touch. His partner in this effort is most importantly his wife Linda. She, more than anyone helped him to realize that a life which fails to give God glory, a life in which we miss the fact that every talent, every gift is God's grace, is a life not worth living. Ceili Rain isn't hiding or "disguising" its Christianity in popular music. No, I think they're trying to tell us that Christ's message can be popular, moving and set to music which parallels the feelings we find in love songs. And they succeed magnificently.

During our television interview, Halligan and Connolly spoke openly about their reliance on God. Songwriter Halligan, in particular, spoke of the difference between being "raised Catholic," and truly believing, practicing and articulating your faith. His personal conversion uses the popularity of contemporary music to proclaim a truth as old as Christ Himself. Buddy Connolly is more laid back, but he too talked about those many times "on the road" when he turns it all over to the Lord in reflective prayer. These guys, and their Ceili Rain band, are stomping musicians who can move a crowd and fire up song, but the message behind the charisma isn't terribly different from what the Apostles first proclaimed: the joy of being in love with God.

And speaking of popular musical groups, have you noticed the phenomenal success of the Backstreet Boys? Not just in America, but around the world, these five guys are touching millions with their music. In the midst of their easy-to-hear music, don't miss the chance to recognize the subtle presence of God's love. In particular, their hit "As Long As You Love Me," could have been written by the Lord Himself if He were singing to the sinners He forgave regularly. "I don't care who you are. Where you're from. What you did; As long as you love me." Tell me that doesn't belong in our reconciliation services! And if you have doubts about the Christian perspective of these colossally attractive young stars, listen to the notes written in their album. Nick Carter, lead singer: "First I'd like to thank God for the talent He has given me." Or how about Howard "Howie D," Dorough: "First and foremost, I'd like to start by thanking our Heavenly Father, for the gift of life and the talent He has given us." Or Alexander James "A.J." McLean: "First and above all I need to thank the Lord for blessing me with my talents, wonderful friends and beautiful family." Or Kevin Richardson: "First and foremost I want to thank God who makes all things possible. My life has been truly blessed." Or the best voice in the group, Brian "B-Rok Littrell, who says: "I can do all things through Christ who gives me strength. Without my Lord and Savior, Jesus Christ, I would not have the gift of song: (or life) to share with you." These were, mind you, just about the most successful singers in America at the moment!

Sometimes folks like to dismiss popular music as a distraction from the things that really matter.

And religious people can be especially judgmental about the corrupting power of popular culture. Just know, there are true Christians out there too.

Ceili Rain and Backstreet Boys are just two of many people in the world of music who know that it all starts and ends in the Lord.

("As Long As You Love Me, " by Max Martin, © Jive Transcontinental Records)

Questions for Reflection

- Did you ever catch yourself thinking of God while listening to a popular love song?
- Can you describe a time when God communicated with you in an unusual way?

Part IV
Loving Relationships

My Friend Joe

OFTEN, when I spend time with my nieces and nephews, they talk about friends from school. Clearly, the ability to have good friends is important to them. And in their relatively young lives they've already discovered that "friend" is an overworked and underlived concept. So in the hope of helping them realize the miraculous gift a true friend can be, I talk to them about my friend Joe.

I met Joe Lukaszewski when we were both in our teens. In very many ways we could not have been more different. And yet, like so many surprises in the ways of love, we became best friends. When I look back on the thirty years we spent together, I realize that Joe lived what are the most basic and absolutely vital elements of friendship.

First, he was a great listener. Joe talked a lot, but he also wanted to hear. And, significantly, he heard the words you said but also understood their deeper (and often unspoken) meaning. He listened with a beautiful combination of his mind, his heart and his soul. And you knew he got what you truly meant by watching his transparently expressive face. I recently had dinner with several friends and realized at the end of the evening that while there was plenty of talking, listening, true listening, was kept at a minimum. Joe would never be guilty of that.

Joe also had the ability to be consistent. A rare jewel in our tenuous world! Joe and I would marvel, every few years, about the wonder of maintaining a constant in the midst of our ever-changing world. We'd grow and change, taking a step up and sometimes a step backwards, but at either end of the journey, there was this beautiful knowledge in recognizing that, win or lose, someone would be there for you.

True friends also challenge. And that's something Joe did regularly. Not with a frontal attack, and never with a lack of kindness. He'd just suggest, ever so gently, that maybe you might want to try another approach in handling this or that.

And since Joe only made these comments after serious reflection, his insight was a jewel. In fact, he was rarely off the mark.

But perhaps most significantly as the basis of true and lasting friendship, Joe loved without conditions. Joe's friends (myself included) could be devoted or not, sensitive to him or not, supportive of him or not, kind to him or not, and in every instance, he'd just love you back no matter what. It was and is the best reflection of God's love I've ever witnessed. Because in a world where people often love you with an assortment of ifs, ands or buts, Joe just loved, period.

A year ago this summer, Joe became ill with a tumor of the brain. He suffered through three traumatic surgeries, chemo and radiation, and the frightening roller coaster of hope and despair when the damned tumor would come back every time and always with greater ferocity. On April 26th, Joe went home to God. Sitting at his grave over at Holy Rood, I find myself galloping through so many emotions. These have included gratitude, anger, incredible sorrow, frustration, and an emptiness that aches worse than any hurt ever has before. Truly, there are days where the loss of this gentle and generous bear of a man has made me wonder. Is it better to love so deeply when the possibility of loss will only cause a wound that stings like no other? Or would it be better to keep our distance, love lightly and spare ourselves this valleylike despair? And then I think of Joe. I remember the richness of his heart, and the part I was privileged to share in that heart, and a smile breaks through even the most fearsome days.

Joe was fond of saying that "friends are the family we choose for ourselves." Now and forever, I will treasure my membership in this good man's family of friends. Thanks, Joe, for being there for me then, now and always.

Question for Reflection

● What are your personal answers to Father Jim's questions about the decision to love deeply or lightly?

Making Sense

MY friend Michael came by for a chat. A great young man of deep sensitivity and intelligence, Michael had a question which troubled him. Recently his Mom died of cancer. She suffered a lot, and Michael saw her through this difficult death. His mother was a wonderful person who genuinely tried to live a good and decent life. So Michael wanted to know the answer to a question many of us ask: why do bad things happen to good people? Or, perhaps, the underlying question might be: why do the wicked often live lives of ease while people of goodness suffer? Michael's question has no easy answer, because it's predicated on human logic. In our lives we believe that if someone is good, we should take care of them and protect them. In these human standards, the bad deserve everything they get. Many people like my friend Michael would like to see God directly intervene in the affairs of humanity. Like the Lone Ranger He should help all the good folks and punish the bad guys. But God has an understanding about life and love that far exceeds our own.

God knows that real and perfect love is lived in freedom, and because He loves us so completely, He refuses to play the puppeteer in our lives. Like the healthy parent, the Lord gives life, encourages, nurtures, blesses and cares for us. But He also knows that part of loving is letting go. So He places us in what potentially can be a perfect world and challenges us to renew the face of the earth.

Could He come in and just make everything right? Well, of course; He is, after all, God! But He knows that it's only the things we achieve for ourselves which truly matter. So, for example, someone in our family can hound us to get him or her a particular birthday gift. And, finally, after a good bit of nagging, we'll give them what they asked for. But that gift can never mean as much as the gift freely given. In the same way, God wants us to make the world the "perfect" place it can be.

He's left us the capacity to do extraordinary things, but it's our job to seek after the good with boundless diligence. So, for example, we can cure cancer. It's been here too long. But we won't beat it without a deep dedication to spending our resources on attaining a cure. In America, we spend more in any given year on Hallmark cards than we do on cancer research. That's just plain disproportionate! Part of our freedom to decide is the necessary wisdom to choose rightly.

Another example comes to mind. The Lord has granted us the insight to harness the incredible power of the atom. This energy has unbounded potential. It can heat and light up worlds once shrouded in darkened coldness. It can also waste humankind. The choice is ours. God leaves us the power and the freedom to decide.

Food offers yet another instance. On the day you read this column, over 20,000 people will die of starvation. At the same time, barns in the USA, and elsewhere, will bulge with unused grain. We have the means to feed the planet, we simply choose to let people die. Is that God's doing, or ours? Of course, it's about our choices and values. There are two million childless couples in America who will seek to adopt this year. Only 50,000 will succeed. At the same time almost two million unborn children will be aborted. Is the fact that so many good people go childless God's fault? Not at all. He gives freedom in love. We choose to spend that freedom foolishly.

So what's the answer to young Michael's painful question? Well, the tough reality is that God loves us enough to let us be free. We can use that freedom to create or destroy, to build or tear down. Sadly, too often we misuse this incredible world we've been given.

During the carnage in Rwanda, the world sat there doing nothing. We could have stopped the killing. But Rwanda, unlike Kuwait, was not of "vital interest" to us. And so we let them die, a million men, women and children. It would be easy to shake our fist in God's face and blame the state of our world on His impotence. It's much harder to look in the mirror and own responsibility for what we're doing to and with our world. And if we look around at all the bad and find ourselves on the verge of tears, know that God weeps, too. He made and entrusts to us a truly beautiful world. And like a parent who sees His child spend incredible potential badly, He would like to make it all better. But, in His wisdom, He knows that that's a job only we can accomplish.

Questions for Reflection

- How do you explain a God who "lets bad things happen to good people"?
- Why is it difficult to own the "unpleasant" circumstances of life?

Sharing Ourselves

I KNOW a man who sits on at least a dozen corporate boards. He's hugely successful and widely respected for his advice and insight. And as he is also devoutly Catholic, it's not surprising that the Church has often tapped him to serve as the chair of many humanitarian efforts. He's a millionaire who, through the Church, tries to give back something for all the blessings he's received.

Over lunch recently, this great man shared some unsettling insights into the Church he loves and serves. I didn't like what I heard but certainly respected his integrity and his right to express some painful opinions. "You know, Father, people in corporate America are often portrayed as cutthroat and mercenary. And, in fact, many of the most successful people in business are without much conscience. But bad as my colleagues can be, they can't hold a candle to some of what you priests do to one another." He then recounted a plethora of stories about priests in positions of authority who "work overtime" to calumnize, backbite, backstab and dismantle other priests. In one of his most stinging rebukes, my friend said, "It's little wonder that the Church is suffering from a lack of vocations; you don't even support your own kind."

His criticism of ways in which priests engage in unkind or uncharitable criticism of other priests reminded me of a moving and eloquent talk offered by Msgr. Jim McNamara, formerly director of the Office of Priest Personnel and the author of a wonderful book called *The Power of Compassion*. Shortly before leaving his personnel duties he warned the clergy of the diocese to be "kinder to each other." He told us that we were much too "hard on one another."

Both Msgr. McNamara and my businessman friend were highlighting an unpleasant but perhaps real phenomenon. And I don't know that it's limited to the priesthood. In fact, the dysfunction of relationships between clergy are probably only a microcosm of the ways in which we relate to the people we share life with on many levels.

Take, for instance, our families. Every week, during parish confessions, people seem to confess the same sins. Most people talk about their failure to love, respect, treasure and be kind to the people who mean the most to them: their families. People recount the manifold ways in which they verbally abuse or emotionally snub the people they love the most. We certainly speak to people in our families more angrily, more critically than we ever speak to the people we see each day at work. I suspect that's because we could never get away with saying the things we say in family to people who are our co-workers. They just wouldn't tolerate the kind of behavior we subject our families to. And yet, these are the people we're supposed to love.

Maybe it's a case of presumption. I mean, most of us recognize that no matter what we do to them, our families are still going to accept us, tolerate us, put up with us, and even continue to love us. And that acceptance can lull us into believing that our unacceptable behavior is, in fact, kind of acceptable. But our lack of kindness, civility and basic decency toward those who are closest to us should embarrass and challenge us. It's never acceptable to tear down anyone, least of all people whom we profess to love.

Taking advantage of the fact that family or personal ties will bind people to tolerate our lack of charity seems to be manipulating the power of love to our own advantage. I recall one day when after an awful day of being drained by others, listening to endless complaints about one thing or another, and being unable or unwilling to give it back to the people who had made the day a misery, I stopped by my parents' home. There I proceeded to pick a fight with my totally innocent mother about something she said which bothered me a bit. Without missing a beat, she wisely put me in my place. "You know,

Jim," she told me, "you're not really mad at me. But if it helps you cope to dump your frustration or anger on me, that's okay. But just know that's what you're doing." Ouch! She scored a bulls-eye on that one.

We are so very tough on people who share our lives, our hearts and our history. They are, on paper, the people we should treasure the most. And yet, in real life, they're the people we're most inclined to dismantle. Be it priests to other priests, or family member to other family member, it's wrong, it's unnecessary; and it's such a waste of the privilege we have to love. Love is not a doormat; it's an invitation to respect, to treasure, to affirm and to encourage—not when people are dead but while they live and share our lives.

Question for Reflection

- We've all had "ouch" moments when we've hurt the ones we love. If recognition is the beginning of healing—list the people you owe an apology to and the ways to avoid a recurrence.

Sharing the Load

MEETING recently with a couple who planned to marry, we got talking about the responsibilities they'd be sharing as spouses and as parents. The young woman, in her early 20s, described a life vision which sounded like a combination of full-time work outside the home and the additional tasks of mother and keeper of the home. When it came time for the groom (about 26) to reflect on his life expectations they centered primarily on the career he'd already begun, and said almost nothing about his domestic responsibilities. In this short conversation were laid, I think, the seeds of future conflict and frustration.

Years ago we lived in an America in which at least one parent was full time around the home. The other worked full time outside the home. But times and situations have changed drastically. Due essentially to financial demands, where there are two-parent homes, both are working outside the home in at least 88 percent of the situations. You'd think, then, that we'd have re-oriented ourselves to the simple fact that two careers means that both will share the burdens of caring for the home and the children. A recent study, however, indicated that we're not embracing that model yet.

In a study of time management, look at how the differences broke out. The areas wherein men and women spent the same time on activities included: sleeping, grooming and dressing, eating at home, eating away, taking transportation to and from work, and non-food shopping. Situations wherein women spent more time on an activity than men included: preparing food, household chores, shopping for food and doing related house-centered errands. Men, on the other hand, beat women on the time they spend on: home entertainment, hobbies, crafts, exercise and sports.

So what's the problem with that breakdown? Well, to begin with, it suggests that there are family-related activities which should be determined by sex. And truth be told, that isn't really accurate. Cooking, cleaning, doing the laundry, buying food, or scrubbing a toilet aren't distinctly male or female tasks. They are, instead, family concerns, human responsibilities.

We do women a great and stressful disservice in expecting them to work full-time outside the home and continue to do the major jobs of running a home as well. Fairness, justice and simple loving concern mean that men have to recognize that home jobs must be shared jobs—that for a home or family to function in 21st century America, every responsibility should be a mutual concern. When young people date, especially when that dating turns serious, a woman needs to look closely at the guy she loves and ask a few simple but important questions. Like, can I see this man sharing the tasks of educating and nurturing our children equally with me? Will he balk at the need to change a diaper, or wash a load of laundry, or scrub out a filmy bathtub? If we both do the eating, is he also willing to share the responsibility of cooking our food? How well does he handle a vacuum? And more to the point: is he so caught up in strict male and female roles, that he can't see that we're in this together?

There are many qualities we should be examining when we consider building a life with someone. And in an age which requires both partners to work outside the home, a spirit of mutual sharing becomes ever more critical. If he thinks you should bring home a paycheck and run a perfect home, and raise a perfect family, without seeing himself in a similar role, maybe you need to put a brake on the relationship and remind him that equal work demands equal responsibility!

Questions for Reflection

- What if any of this hit home for you?
- Consider the marriages among your family and friends. Which ones are positive role models for you in sharing home jobs?

What's Important?

I THINK I became aware of the hat last summer. On a cruise up the inner passage of Alaska, it seemed to never leave his head. The head belonged to my 13-year-old nephew Matthew. The hat in question was and is a standard-issue baseball cap. That's when I became most fully aware of the teen-age obsession with hats, hat head and America's love for baseball headgear. Coming back to New York, I started to look more closely at the heads of young people everywhere. And sure enough, eight out of ten were wearing the hat. On their heads during the trip to school. Off for the school day, then right back on once the last school bell sounded.

It's interesting. Ask most teenagers what's important and surveys tell us they respond "independence." But when it comes to questions of clothing or style, they tend to lose their independence and follow the trend. And baseball hats are decidedly a popular trend.

Sometimes that trend, that sense of the popular, runs contrary to what's good, what's safe and what's sensible. Let me mention an example. Most teens, at least until they get a license, need transportation. That need is usually fulfilled by the use of a bike. For a period of about five years, it's the necessary transportation of choice. Now, there's a way to look as you ride your bike; and, at present, it involves the omnipresence of the aforementioned baseball hat. Check out the bike riders passing you by on any given day. Chances are, they're wearing the hat. And they're probably enjoying the look of wearing the hat as well.

But then we run into a problem. It's called state law. Because after years of cracked skulls, several thousand a year, the government has mandated that young people riding bikes must wear helmets. Helmets, while they may save your brain from permanent damage, look nerdy. No self-respecting cool person of teen-age persuasion wants to be caught wearing one around a friend or neighbor. On one hand you've got your life and well-being. On the other you've got your look, your reputation and your concern about what other people might say about you. For parents, there's no contest. The heads of the children they've worked mightily to raise are far more important than being cool or not. But to many teens, concerned about acceptance, popularity and fitting in, the helmet is a short route to social rejection. Logic flies out the window. Safety takes a back seat to effect.

I've observed this conflict in close proximity as my sister and my nephew debate the helmet vs. the baseball cap question. Safety vs. the look. And, truth be told, my nephew finds the helmet oppressive. For my sister it's about protecting an object of love, peer acceptance be damned. Now, some kids try to have it both ways. I know teenagers who dutifully wear the helmet until they're out of parental eyeshot, then pitch the helmet and smash on the beloved baseball cap. Dishonest, but seemingly a way of keeping everyone happy. My nephew, fortunately I think, can't see his way clear to doing that. He sees that as lying, and somewhere along the way he's grown (happily) uncomfortable with that choice. So the battle, the debate, goes on.

In many ways I see the hat question as a model for every parent-teen conflict likely to develop over the next few years. Because whether it's a baseball cap or a curfew, a beer or a cigarette, a sexual activity or a bad choice of friends and companions, the fundamental issue is the same. Do we do what in our guts we know is right and good, moral and safe; or do we do what will gain us (however fleeting) the acceptance and popularity of our peer friends?

I have no easy answers, but I will tell you this. I see my friends from high school a few times a year. I like them a lot; but they can't begin to compare to the long-term reliance, trust, and love I share with my folks.

The momentary or the long-range? A tough choice; but I've got to believe that in his heart, my nephew knows his mom is right. And that she'll be there for him long after the bike and the baseball hat have been relegated to the back of the garage.

I like baseball caps, too. But I like the heads underneath them more.

(Author's note: With all the bashing TV takes, it's good to recommend something everybody in the family can watch—and learn from. Warner Brothers television, Channel 11, offers such a program on Monday nights. It's called "Seventh Heaven." It stars Stephen Collins as a minister, who is a father and husband. The values it presents are terrific. Give it a try.)

Question for Reflection

- If a "safe risk" is only an oxymoron, what can help you to decide when to draw the line between safe and sorry.

Family Reunion

MY sister Joan noticed it at Uncle Bob's funeral: that in recent years, our family only seems to get together when someone dies. And important as it is to be there for each other in times of loss, she figured it would be better to enjoy the living years together. So Joan organized a family reunion. It was a great success, bringing together a wide variety of personality types and ages. The youngest attendee was a month old, the oldest was 85. All shared a Lisante heritage. Each also came to get to know their family a little better.

From my perspective it was a revealing experience. People saw me as "the family priest." Some thought they had to treat me with great deference and respect. They approached me as if I were from another planet. So, for example, one relative told a story and slipped by mentioning the word "damn." He immediately apologized for uttering the word in my presence. He should only know that at some of the pro-life demonstrations I attend, words of far greater "color" are regularly shot at people in Roman collars from our pro-choice counterparts! There were others who, not knowing me, but having some acquaintance with the Church, wanted to talk shop. So they would tell me all about their parish priests, or Sisters, or festivals, or children's Masses. In one case an out-of-state relative asked me if I knew "Father Paul." I asked her his last name. She didn't know it. I asked where he was from. She said she thought he came from Michigan. I told her, no, I don't know Father Paul. She looked at me quizzically and said, "I thought you all knew each other."

But the most moving encounters were with those who have no real experience of Church. These are relatives who gave up on the Church a long time ago—either because they thought that they were not welcome or because they thought their lives were somehow not "good enough" to be a part of the community we call the Catholic Church. Several of these folks had been divorced and remarried outside the Church. Some were living with boyfriends; others hadn't been to the sacraments in more years than they cared to remember. Still others, while they pray privately, are suspicious of the institutional Church for being what they term "too political."

There were, of course, others who offered some pretty lame excuses for their time away from Church. One told me that he disliked the "changes" in the Church. He liked the old Mass better. So I told him about the fact that Mass is still offered in Latin in some churches. With that excuse removed, he tried another. "They talk too much about money in the church." I started to realize that it wasn't about money or a Latin Mass, this guy just didn't want to bother getting to church.

But for every cynic, there were other experiences of great promise. People who want to come back. People who feel incomplete without Mass and the sacraments. People who feel that they've left behind a great richness when they stopped being active in their faith. People who truly want to come home. A lot of my relatives took down my phone number at the end of the party. They said they'd be in touch. They said they needed to talk about how they might get "back to Church." I hope they really call. And I hope that I have the patience and ability to walk the walk with them back to this Church we love. Because my family reunion reminded me that evangelization isn't just a word. It's a role of invitation we're all called to live, inviting people we care about to "come and see" the wonders of our faith.

Questions for Reflection

- We open our homes, share our food and deep thoughts with those we love. Do we love them enough to try to bring them home to Church?

- How can you invite your non-practicing loved ones to take another look?

Do It Today

DAVID Mahoney has been my friend for over thirty years. We met one summer at camp and stayed in touch by phone, by letter and through infrequent visits. David lived in Worcester, Massachusetts; and so he'd drive down about once a year. I tried to return the visit whenever time allowed. David is dear to me for many reasons, not the least of which is his early and constant support for my vocation. He was one of the first to suggest that I might be called to serve people as a priest. We never talked without him encouraging me, affirming my life journey and promising to pray for me and support me with his friendship.

David was a postal worker and spent too many years pounding the pavement. Inevitably, his body took a beating. In recent years, his back and hips have become a mess. He needed surgery and stopped working about four years ago. Nothing seemed to relieve his discomfort. We'd talk about his plight, and I could sense that with each passing month his will to live diminished. I invited David to my installation as a pastor; but it took him such energy just to get up and move about his apartment, a trip to New York was out of the question. But David being David, he made sure to call the monks at St. Joseph's Abbey in Spencer and order a vestment for me to wear. Such was his innate generosity and goodness.

Afterwards David called my rectory and left a message, wondering how the installation had gone and asking if I'd received the vestment he sent. Late Saturday night I heard the answering machine and sensed that he sounded incredibly tired. I made a mental note to call him during the week. He called again on Sunday, sounding even weaker. A few days later I returned his call and got no answer. The next morning I received a call from Brother Anthony of St. Joseph's Abbey, informing me that David Mahoney had passed away in his sleep, that his pain was over.

I tell you this story to tell you about a beautiful man who enriched my life; to tell you about how important encouragement and affirmation are in all of our lives; to tell you about how even distance can't quash a true friendship. But I also tell this story in a spirit of regret. I will always miss David, and I will always be sorry that I allowed the "busy-ness" of life to keep me from returning his call. I had a million good excuses; and, after all, I think I knew a bit of what David would say. We'd probably talk about his aches and pains, and I'd been there so many times before. But this time was special. He was nearing the end of his life's journey, and he needed a patient and attentive friend to listen and to care. I wasn't and should've been there for him.

Death, we know, comes for us all. But being procrastinators, we tend to believe that it's coming for others, not for us and our loved ones. But St. Paul writes that the Lord may well come "like a thief in the night," stealing into our lives when we least expect it. If I'd known David was going home to God, I'd have been more present. But that's the point, we never know. And so it becomes our duty to minister to one another, to care for each other, to love one another, not later, not tomorrow, not next week, but today.

On the morning after David died, I was celebrating an early morning Mass. In the homily, I shared the story of my missed opportunity to love and serve my friend David. At the door of the church, a woman stopped to thank me for sharing my own sorrow. Seems she has two friends who are closing in on the end of their earthly lives, and she's been putting off a visit because she too is just "too busy." She mentioned that she'd be calling her friends that day and setting up a time to get together. Her promise left me with a smile because if David's death can be a wake-up call, a gentle reminder that "now is the acceptable time" for us to do the good we always intend to do, then maybe other loved ones won't have to be left untended.

In each of our lives there are words unspoken, hurts unresolved, pains we intend one day to fix, calls that we mean to make, friends and family we intend to tell about how much we love and appreciate them. Please don't delay. Pick up the phone. Drop in. Send that card or letter. Make that first effort (even if it runs contrary to your pride). And do it today. David understands all things now. So he knows about my love, my caring, my gratitude and my appreciation for his presence in my life. But you know what? I wish I'd told him anyway.

Questions for Reflection

- Think about a wake up call you've had recently.
- In the future, what can you do to get there before the alarm goes off?

Life: The Fragile Gift

TRAVELING to the Diocese of Palm Beach some four years ago, I journeyed in "civilian" clothes. But as we arrived at the airport, I knew that the folks who had invited me to speak wouldn't know me without "the collar." So as the majority of passengers quickly exited, I took some time to transform myself into my priestly look! That made me the last passenger to exit. Not wanting to make my hosts fear for my absence, I galloped to the terminal. As I ran too quickly I failed to navigate a sharp turn and found myself bumping into a couple equally determined to get on the plane heading back to New York.

Knocking into someone is always a little awkward, but this time it was more so because it was John Kennedy, Jr. and his intended, Carolyn Bessette. All of us shared a little blame and we were all mutually apologetic. I think they were a little more patient with me owing to the clerical collar. We chatted a bit and they were, as now everyone testifies, sweet, unaffected and gracious people. They were also so closely linked that the two looked to be one person, very obviously in love.

Which caused me to mention that on that very day the New York tabloids were trumpeting their probable break-up, owing to a now-famous spat in Central Park. I told them it was good to see that the tabloids had it wrong. To which John remarked: "They absolutely did," looking into her eyes with a look that said "I adore you." Wishing each other a less bumpy day, we went our separate ways. When I met him, I thought he was legendary. As I left him, I was amazed at the similarity between Carolyn and John and every engaged couple who've sat across the desk from me, planning their wedding. Two very normal people, grateful for the opportunity to have found a soulmate, a best friend, a companion for life's journey.

So what, then, should we make of their untimely death? That it was a tragic, senseless and powerfully sad moment.

That it reminds us, yet again, that there is no lasting protection from death for anyone. That in death, we are all to face the same God, carrying with us only the good we've done. That life is a precious and fleeting gift meant to be lived fully and with a spirit of thanksgiving. That we should take time to celebrate the people we love and see them as the gifts we'll one day ache for, but today too often take for granted.

The death of John and Carolyn Kennedy and her sister Lauren also reminds us about the anchor of faith. In this sadness, as in every one before, the Kennedys turn to prayer, to the Mass, to their enduring faith. You may (as I do) have your political differences with this clan, but you can't help but admire their obvious reliance on the power of faith, especially in times of trial.

What I don't believe this death tells us is that the Kennedys (or anyone for that matter) are "cursed." To believe in such nonsense essentially makes a joke out of the merciful love and forgiveness demonstrated time and time again by Jesus. It echoes the notion of the Lord as a "gotcha God" who looks for us to fail so He can punish the sinful. That may be some people's God, but it isn't the God of Catholic Christianity.

I would hope that the shortened lives of people like these would remind us that human life is fragile and perilously vulnerable. Maybe that awareness can make us less given to the verbal violence and physical disrespect we discover in each day's news.

Question for Reflection

● What important lessons have you learned through your losses?

A Wonderful Life

WHEN I was seminarian, and thought about the priests I knew from parish life, young priests were the newly ordained. That meant five years or under. Guys who were out fifteen or more years were, I thought, galloping toward dinosaur status. So imagine my shock, horror and surprise at recently celebrating nineteen years of priesthood! Where did the years go?

The first five years were charmed. I worked in a terrific parish, a place called St. Boniface. I had a wonderful boss, Msgr. Peter Ryan, and associates I admired and emulated. The people there considered me "the kid" priest, and delighted in every forward growth or development. Then came a different kind of assignment, eleven years in a specialized ministry. The diocesan Office of Family Ministry confronted so many "hot button" issues: divorce and separation, abortion and euthanasia, preparation for marriage, Natural Family Planning, bereavement and marital healing. It was exhilarating, challenging, controversial, and a constant learning experience.

Then, four years ago, I re-entered parish life as the pastor of my home community. And in many ways it's been the most beautiful of all experiences. No longer young, the parishioners don't hang on your every word, nor are they any longer entranced by the cuteness of your mistakes.

As a priest, you quickly learn that they've seen people like us come and go, but they're in it for the long run. It's humbling to sense their devotion and absolute loyalty. It also reminds you that your vision of where the parish should be is meaningless unless it's rooted in an understanding of their permanent status as residents of the local community. I'm reminded, for instance, of the time in St. Boniface when I preached on racial tolerance. The community was becoming swiftly integrated with many diverse cultures and colors. From my lofty perch (as a temporary resident), I suggested that everyone should accept all the new people moving into town. One day a lifer gave it to me directly: "You priests are good at telling us how to live in community But you rarely stay very long. You might have more credibility if you invested in this parish like we have, for life!" Her point was well taken. People "passing through" should be cautious about confidently telling people how to live their lives. It's a lesson I've tried to remember in my current parish, St. Thomas the Apostle. Move forward, yes. But remember and respect the past and those who will be our communities' future long after I've gone.

Parish life teaches every day. It's helped me to know that:

—It's all God's work. There are days when you get tired, depressed, and feel no particular comfort in the message you're preaching. Then you stand at the back door saying good-bye to your people. Someone comes up and says: "Thank you for that homily. It was just what I needed today." And you scratch your head wondering, what did I say and where did the good come from? Then you start to get it. It's not our words, or our insight. It's about how He uses us. And He uses us for the good in ways we'd never expected.

—Saying it isn't as important as living it. I used to think that being articulate was very important, that the way you said something was the earmark of success or failure. And, yes, it's important to try to speak well. But more and more I see another truth. There are times, especially as people experience death, when what you say means far less than just being there. A hug, a hand on the shoulder, a tear shared with a grieving family is far more important and real than paragraphs of eloquence.

—Celibacy. I have a friend named Luca. He runs the local pizzeria. He's born in Italy and is a true friend. But celibacy blows his mind. In fact, he just doesn't believe it at all. "Don't tell me you guys don't all fool around," insists my pizza buddy. "No one can live without sex." Well, Luca, it isn't always easy, but it is possible to let go of physical intimacy. What's impossible to forego is the need for love. And, happily, the longer I live my priesthood, the more I feel the incredible and giving love of people for their priests. And that loving assurance makes all the difference.

—People are the Church. It's amazing what we priests don't know. I never realized how ignorant I was until I became a pastor. You're expected to understand bigtime finances, but without any training. You're expected to know about physical structures, leaking roofs, cracked sidewalks and the vicissitudes of asbestos. You want to feed your people spiritually, but have a congregation including people who have vastly different needs and aspirations. And then you ask for help.

It's always there. People are so good, so generous. They don't expect you to know everything, they only want you to say you need assistance. They're there and they make it all happen with untiring dedication. I am, every day, amazed by the time and talent and generosity of my people.

On the chalice my parents gave me eighteen years ago is an engraving of Jesus and His Apostles. It's an image of the Last Supper. These men were, we know, weak, foolish, terribly human, cowardly, insincere, full of themselves and yet called. It's so comforting and encouraging to know that as apostle or priest, our Lord and His people make up for our lack and weakness. This truly is a wonderful life.

Questions for Reflection

- Out of all the points Msgr. Jim makes about his life as a priest, which struck you as "wonderful."
- List some of the "wonderful" things about your life.

The Family Mango

VISITING Rome for the beatification of Padre Pio gave me the opportunity to go shopping. No, not for me but for my church! Because nowhere will you find finer religious vestments and other items we need for worship. I'd been told that one of the very best stores for religious articles was called Mango, located on the Via Del Mascherino. In truth, I found some outstandingly fine things, but none to compare to the beauty of the family named Mango.

This is truly a family business. Mom and Dad (Anna Maria and Mario), supported by two beautiful daughters (Paola and Daniella) are accompanied by their beloved son and brother Maurizio. They work six days a week, morning until night, taking off only on Sunday. They are driven by a natural work ethic, but also by something more vital: their love for someone in the family who is sick.

Maurizio is 25 years old. He is charismatic and filled with joy. Several years ago, he visited America and studied at Molloy College in Rockville Centre. From that experience, he has a passing knowledge of English and a surpassing love of life. He is the star of this family, the youngest and the most treasured. Several years ago, following his return to Italy, Maurizio grew ill. His bodily coordination betrayed him, his hands and legs shaking unsteadily. His condition, taking on a steady palsy-like imbalance, turned his world upside down. The diagnosis, after a myriad of tests, was bleak. Maurizio suffers from a degenerative atrophy of the brain stem. The motor for all bodily functions is slowly and irretrievably breaking down. Maurizio is one smart guy, he knows that means that life is diminishing. His family was, understandably, devastated. But beyond the shock and horror of the news, they rallied. It has cost them dearly, but they have no regrets.

The business had been run by an extended family, Mario's brothers shared the ownership. But these same brothers were uncomfortable about the in-store presence of the physically challenged nephew. They would have preferred that he be kept home, hidden away. Maurizio's family would not hear of it. Instead, pooling all their collective resources, they bought the brothers out. They would not hide their son because he was different. Weak or well, he is still their Maurizio. In Paola's case, the sacrifice was romantic. Her boyfriend of many years didn't like the time and effort spent on her little brother. His care was an inconvenient drag on their dating relationship. Some might have sidestepped a fading brother in favor of a romantic future. Not Paola. She gave her boyfriend his walking papers. A brother, she figured, was for always and not to be dismissed by anyone. If someone who said he loved her expected that she could forfeit her love of and attention to a sick brother, then that suitor need look elsewhere for his companion .

Maurizio is progressively unsteady, so they've put him in charge of the cash register, a sitting position which preserves his dignity. And, yes, I did see customers who looked mildly uncomfortable at the sight of his shaking body. But there is no sense of embarrassment or discomfort from Maurizio's family. He is completely "normal" to them, as seen with the eyes of love.

There is clearly heartbreak facing this wonderful family. The doctors give little hope for Maurizio's recovery. And he, rather than demanding a miracle, seems so humble before his future. When I asked him if he desired prayers for a cure, he gently declined. "There are," said Maurizio, "so many people suffering in the world, so many people with greater pains than mine. Why should God bother to address my needs?" Instead of direct divine intervention, the family Mango works to offer Maurizio a lived experience of God's comforting presence.

I was struck by their heroic efforts at normalcy. To walk, Maurizio must be supported by a brace of two family members, one under each arm. They act as if this were the ordinary way in which people move across the sidewalk. At dinner one night other diners seemed to gape at the family as they eased Maurizio through a crowd, seemingly oblivious to the stares. Of course Maurizio's family recognized the looks of bewilderment. But they have a value more precious than gold. They have decided to love their son and brother best by letting him feel the embrace of a family who will let him live and die with dignity, with respect, with a sense of appreciation and with the absolute knowledge that he is treasured and beloved.

As American culture grapples with the Kervorkians, wondering about the value of assisted suicide, mercy killing, and euthanasia, I saw what is, I think, the real solution to those who suffer irreversible illness. It's the acknowledgment that we're all going to die, and so we should help each other to live with grace and peace and love. I learned that in the shadow of the Vatican, on a small street called Via Del Mascherino, watching and admiring the family Mango.

Question for Reflection

● What are some of the ways that families with physically challenged members become opportunities of grace for others?

Truths That Last

NO matter how long you live, there are some lessons you never forget. One is a message they give you in "Driver's Education class that's never left my head.

They instruct you to remember that when holding the steering wheel, you should think of the wheel like the face of a clock. And your right hand should always be at two o'clock, while your left hand's located at the equivalent of ten o'clock. That's supposed to give you the best control over the car.

Most of us are fastidious about holding the wheel as instructed during Driver's Ed class and throughout the driving test. Then something amazing happens. We get the letter in the mail telling us that we've passed and, almost overnight, our hands slip to the bottom of the wheel. Then we get really cocky and start driving with one hand. Some of my friends reduce that hold to a single finger!

I remember that several years after getting my license I was also a member of the "finger-steering" brigade. Then one night, far from home, I was smack in the middle of a driving and blinding snow storm. On one of the trickier parkway exits, I lost control of the car. It started spinning and I was certain all was lost. I can't remember how I responded to the loss of control. But I do know that in the end, I was okay. I also remember that once the car stopped I looked at my hands which had, miraculously, returned to their correct place, at two and ten o'clock. Crisis will do that. It returns your focus to the right way. Being tossed and spun around has a way of reminding us of truths we learned a long time ago. Truths that last.

Lent is supposed to be a time in which we return to the ways that work, the ways of goodness, the path which leads us to be our best selves. And it's not a season reserved exclusively for adult Catholics. It's for everyone.

So many of the lessons we learned as kids were, are, and always will be true. We think we've outgrown them but we don't. That reality became clear to me as I watched the Barbara Walters interview with Monica Lewinsky. All the old truths were there, and it was a great lesson in moral living. For example?

So many of our parents warn us to pick our friends carefully. But, in fact, we choose carelessly. We often replace our parents and family with friends who are unworthy of the trust we give them. Monica did that when she blurted out her story not just to Linda Tripp, but to a dozen other "friends" who quickly sold her story out. Monica mistook a listening ear for a sensitive heart. She got burned badly. So do we all when we place our lives in the hands of unworthy or untrustworthy "friends."

Parents! teachers and priests regularly tell teens that sex is holy and good, but that it's meant to be shared in the right time, in the right place and with the right person. That means your spouse. Nonetheless, young people often share it with a passing passion.

The passion is spent and so, too often is the relationship. That's what Monica did. She confused passion for love and was left with a broken heart. When asked how she felt now after being discarded by President Clinton, she admitted feeling "dirty, used and angry." Maybe we should listen to the folks who've been around the block a few times. Maybe we should treasure sex and guard its use carefully, thinking with our heads and hearts and souls.

Another eternal truth: every lie catches up with you. Monica found that out too. In a misguided attempt to protect herself, her family and the man she thought she loved, she told a whopper. And, boy, did it come back to haunt her. You can never go wrong by telling the truth.

Monica's story also tells us a lot about consequences. She never seemed to understand those. Feeling angry and rejected by the President; she sought the sexual comfort of a guy named

Tom. But she was clearly not ready for any serious relationship. She needed time to heal and that meant living chastely. Monica thought failed sex could be made better by more sex. She was wrong. Rebound relationships (we learned long ago) almost always die a bad death. This one did too. Monica ended up getting pregnant with Tom and then having the baby aborted. So not only did her heart die twice, but a child had to die before Monica could remember that moral choices always have consequences—something she probably heard before but never took to heart.

When we learn to drive, we learn lifesaving basics. When we learn to live, we learn life saving basics. In both cases we think we know better than the lessons we learned. We don't. It's time to put our hands and our lives back in the two and ten o'clock positions.

Question for Reflection

● Sometimes our lives seem to be spinning "out of control" and we need to get a firm grip on the "truths that last." What makes it so difficult "to go out and do the right thing" as Dr. Laura unceasingly advises her callers?

Bachelor Party

IT seems like a perfect wedding. Imagine a couple, who might be called Suzanne and Brad. Planning to marry, they come to see me, and they're literally glowing with love. They're in their mid-twenties, strikingly attractive, clearly delighted with each other.

Such a couple would be meticulous in making plans for their wedding day, and their wedding ceremony would be beautiful to watch and meaningful to listen to. People would walk away from the experience comfortable in the fact that providence had smiled on our happy newlyweds, that each had found the proper "soulmate."

Imagine, then, the shock and dismay I would feel to find them coming for a visit, as little as a year later, to discuss dissolution of the marriage. What could have gone wrong?

Well, far too often, I've seen couples whose relationship was already suffering by their wedding day from a hidden cancer. And that malignancy was caused by lies and poor judgment.

For eons, about-to-be married men have gathered for a custom which, of itself, doesn't have to be bad. No, bachelor parties as a celebration of transition, as a time for the guys to gather and congratulate a friend's good fortune in finding someone to love, are perfectly valid. But that's not what they've become. In growing case after case they represent one final opportunity to be a jerk. With heavy reliance on alcohol (and sometimes drug) consumption, and with a skewered appreciation for lustful sexual encounters "friends" are giving their engaged companion the chance for a final fling. Some have confessed that they participate because it's "the last time" they can "do it" before marriage ties them down.

And that's exactly what happened to my friend Brad. He allowed himself to buy into the concept of infidelity as a last hurrah, as a final treat before the altar. A week before his wedding he cooperated with the temptation offered by his bachelor party companions. They provided a woman, and he engaged in a terribly compromising act. Unknown to Brad, the visitor left him with unseeable fallout. The marriage took place. Brad and Suzanne shared conjugal bliss, and four months later discovered they also shared an STD (sexually transmitted disease), the remnant of Brad's one-night stand.

Trust, confidence and intimacy die with the advent of the disease. Suzanne would ask, correctly, how Brad could share himself with another woman on the eve of their most sacred promise? Brad would have no answer. It wouldn't be something he could logically explain. He'd know his actions made no rational sense. He had taken a beautiful trust and an outstanding friendship and compromised it for the momentary desire for physical pleasure.

In our increasingly liberated world, it's become fashionable to suggest that old taboos are meaningless. In particular, that sex outside of marriage is so prevalent that it's without serious or long-term consequence. And while that sounds convincing, it's really one more big lie. There is no such thing as sex without consequence: physical, emotional and spiritual. Because deep in our consciences, in the place where we truly value what matters, we want sex for the right reasons. We want it as a sign of friendship. We want it as a mark of closeness and trust. We want it to be unique, to be exclusive. And we want it to be life-giving. Compromised sexual intimacy works to counteract each of these wants. It undermines and often destroys a beautiful and treasured bond. Sometimes the compromised relationship can be saved (the marital healing program called Retrouvaille has been especially effective in this regard), but it is always different.

Two very public compromises of the gift of sexual intimacy reveal the frontal damage of infidelity. By many standards, President Clinton's leadership has been perceived as successful. He might have completed two terms in office with his head held high. Instead, he thrashes about with embarrassment, vainly trying to explain or justify sex outside of his marriage. At one level, you'd think America could care less. After all, some reason, if his policies succeed, who cares about his "personal life?" But we know better. We know that personal compromises of significant relationships also suggest a character unworthy of trust on other issues of national import. Put more bluntly: if you'll lie about this, what else do you lie about?

Or we can consider the tragic life and death of Princess Diana for additional consequences of sexual infidelity. With each new book or article written, it becomes crystal clear that her marriage faded in direct proportion to Prince Charles' unwillingness to forfeit his mistress Camilla Parker Bowles. The dissolution of Charles and Diana's relationship had its genesis in the Prince's naive belief that he could have it both ways, marriage and something on the side. Poor fool.

Liberation has not changed the basics. Sex is innately an act of trust and self-giving. In our guts we know it's meant to be shared carefully. I wish I had a dollar for every man or woman who, confessing marital infidelity, also revealed the stomach pit-nausea they felt after their compromise. That queasy feeling, that momentary sickness, is the alarm clock of our truest selves. It's the part of us that knows that sex is good, holy, Divine. That it's meant to be shared with someone who really matters. That it can't be shared without consequences.

Questions for Reflection

- What will it take to save Suzanne and Brad's marriage?
- Does the expression "being tied down" reflect your thoughts about marriage?

Part V

21st Century Living

Know Your Faith

THE last summer of the century gave me a chance to tour the American heartland, journeying to South Dakota, Minnesota and Michigan. In each state I had the chance to speak and to listen. What I heard was both encouraging and unsettling.

On the positive side, by a long shot, was a visit to the diocese of Sioux Falls, South Dakota. Under the dynamic leadership of Bishop Robert Carlson, the local church held its principle anticipatory celebration of the upcoming millennium. Combining large-scale opportunities for adult education, teen and young adult renewal, communal prayer and social situations which celebrated family life, this diocesan Church challenged many thousands to examine the true meaning of Christ's coming. It inspired Church people (and the unchurched) to take the faith seriously and bring it into real-life situations. It encouraged Catholic Christians to avoid compartmentalizing gospel values into those we can choose to live and those we're free to ignore.

The closing Mass, which followed on an awe-inspiring concert by Christian and popular singer Kathy Trocolli (Long Island native), brought throngs of Catholics into a full-throated proclamation of the uniqueness of our faith. I was especially impressed that Bishop Carlson's ability at bridge-building helped him to get the NBC affiliate to air the entire Mass on network television. If every diocese managed to celebrate the 2,000-year history of our faith with equal zeal, we could truly renew America. So alive was the spirit of renewal in South Dakota, that I met pastors who once enjoyed only 40 percent attendance by Catholics at Mass, and now found 80 percent of their people crowding the churches!

On another leg of my midwest sojourn, I encountered a less attractive side of the Christian personality. I met up with and debated a series of fundamentalist Christians. And let me admit up front that I had a long-standing appreciation for my friends in the Evangelical Churches which stems from our cooperative efforts in the pro-life cause. But this time I saw another face of this way of being Christian. My debate opponents put it bluntly: Catholics, they say, aren't saved and aren't going to heaven. They said we weren't even Christians. Our Pope, they charged, is the anti-Christ and we blaspheme by our "worship" of Mary, the mother of Jesus. Their attacks were both ignorant and self-defeating. To begin with, it seems sad somehow that any Christian Church has to build itself up by knocking another Christian Church down. Why can't the goodness of their perspective work to invite others? Why create a bogeyman in the Catholic Church? When pushed they inevitably ran to the Bible, for them the only thing you need. And they are amazing in their startling ability to rattle off verse after verse. In their "grab bag" and unscientific approach to the Word of God, they find simple answers to life's complexities. Of course they're missing a big crack in their armor. They at the same time proclaim the Catholic faith a "false Church," while acknowledging that the Bible is their all. But who do they imagine selected the books of the Bible as the revealed truth of God? You got it, the Catholic Church did. So if we're as "false" as they claim, why is their faith built on a book our forebears put together?

I found it particularly disconcerting that so many of these fundamentalist Churches prey on Catholic people to up their numbers. They figure, correctly, that many Catholics don't know their faith very well and will probably fold when exposed to the simplicity of twisted scriptural interpretation. And that's where these anti-Catholic fundamentalists need to be stopped; in the renewal of our own people. Places like Sioux Falls are building an informed community of Catholic faith which is far less likely to fall for the corny sales of fundamentalist Christians.

By the way, in preparing to dialog with the Bible literalists, I found two helpmates. Both writings are current and available. One is called *Crossing the Tiber* by Stephen K. Ray. It journeys through one evangelical Protestant's discovery of the Catholic Church. Published by Ignatius Press of San Francisco, it's an excellent point-by-point refutation of much of the anti-Catholic rant we hear from those who would misinterpret our Church and her teachings. Equally valuable is a pamphlet published by Liguori Publications (based in Liguori, Missouri). It's called "Have You Been Saved?" Father Dowling refutes the fundamentalist notion that Catholics are beyond salvation, and he does it using the power of Scripture. Order them from your local Catholic bookstore and read them. You'll never feel ill equipped in the face of evangelical fervor again!

Question for Reflection

● For most Catholics today, it's important to keep up with politics, the economy, and the latest in sports and entertainment. Why isn't keeping up with their faith a priority?

Driving Safely

THERE'S a man from my parish who always sits in the front pew at daily Mass. He's blessed with a truly beatific countenance. When he prays, there's this incredible aura of holiness about him. I think most people envy his spiritual glow. Hold on to that image.

During the Christmas holidays, I found myself a few gifts short. Deciding that the Massapequa Mall was my best bet, I shot down a single-lane road known as Route 107. In front of me was a car moving at what I viewed as a snail's pace. Having only two hours to do my shopping, I decided that I had to get around this driver. In a stupid and impulsive move, I moved into the oncoming lane of traffic, planning to scoot around the slowpoke driver and move along my merry way. But as happens when we're sure there's no oncoming traffic, sure enough another car came barreling at me from the opposite direction. With no time to spare, I veered to my right and got back into my original lane. Not only did I give the oncoming driver a bad scare, but I also managed to drive the poor slow driver off to the side of the road. Suddenly, Mr. slowpoke came alive. Livid with rage, he sped up to my bumper, honking his horn and flashing his brights. Not content with this signal of anger, he then moved his car next to mine, driving in the oncoming lane of traffic. He was clearly furious with me and needed to express that pique. Our eyes met, his lips uttered what looked like a well-known expletive, and then he gave me the finger. Another second passed before our eyes really locked. And then the recognition. This guy was the holy man from Church! In that moment, he too recognized his driving nemesis as the local priest. His face took on a look of shock and immediate remorse. I really felt bad for him and wondered how I should relieve his obvious embarrassment. So I smiled over at his crestfallen face and gave him a blessing. Nothing like returning a sign of the cross for the famed finger! The next morning we faced each other after Mass with mutual discomfort. He for his finger, me for being the dumbest driver in town.

But I'll bet the scene I just described isn't unique to the two of us. Truth is, bad driving seems to be epidemic. And the roads are where too many folks vent a host of unresolved angers. That's dangerous for everyone because when we get behind the wheel of a car, we're not only engaging a vehicle, we're also taking over an instrument of incredible power, a machine which can kill. Over 50,000 Americans will die this year in car accidents. Most of the killer accidents will have been preventable. Many will be related to our tempers, our distractions, our impatience and our over-extended lifestyles. Underneath us are several tons of metal power, easily able to mow down anyone in our path.

We're very sensitive to the dangers in gun possession. We guard them jealously because we recognize them as potential killers. A car can do the same thing. It's a power for good, but also a power for heartbreak. Organizations like MADD and SADD have done a terrific job at sensitizing us to the risks of drunk driving. But maybe we also need to remember that driving "under the influence" isn't limited to drugs and alcohol. Every time we drive, we need to check our moods, our attitudes and our angers. During my Christmas shopping, I was lucky. It could have gone another way. And instead of celebrating a season of new birth, I might have been helping to make it a season of sadness and death. The man from church and I were deeply foolish; please avoid our example. Drive with love and care; it really is a matter of life and death.

Questions for Reflection

- How do your moods affect your driving?
- Can you dial and drive safely?

Misusing Symbols

NBC's "Dateline" program once highlighted a sad and disturbing story about teenagers from California. Seems that four fairly regular guys, all from middle-income homes, all with fairly mainstream families, decided to have a little "fun" in one of their cars. So the four rode through their city bashing, with their attendant baseball bat, cars, mailboxes and some poor souls who happened by on bicycles. To add to their sick pleasure, they also videotaped their exploits. But it gets worse. Buying a gun which sprays paint, they drove through town aiming their gun at the faces of pedestrians. They shot, frightened and harmed several people.

The "Dateline" program focused on the growing violence among teenagers in America from all socio-economic backgrounds. They also interviewed a number of teenagers who, on viewing the videotape, found the damage done by these young men to be "funny" and "cool." When challenged by the reporter, most justified this kind of activity by crediting it to "peer pressure." They suggested that standing against such random violence would cause young people to "lose face."

There was one aspect of this story which troubled me in a particular way. The video revealed that on the rear-view mirror of the car used by these guys, hung an unmistakable pair of rosary beads. In an interview with one of the young men, a fellow named Anthony (the owner and driver of the car), it became clear that he hailed from a Catholic family. Now it will come as no surprise to anyone that Catholics, like people of every religion, commit crimes. But it is especially troubling when Catholics who act in a way which is diametrically opposed to everything our faith stands for, flaunt their Catholicity through the use of religious symbols.

Religious symbols include a number of items. Certainly the rosary is one important example, as are crucifixes, statues of saints, scapulars, religious art and anything which includes an image of Our Lord, or those who consecrate their lives to Him. These symbols or articles exist not as an end in themselves, but rather as a way to direct our attention to the good, to the holy, to the Lord. They are not some kind of hip fashion statement. They should reflect an interior disposition which reverences God and His people.

So, for example, it is completely contradictory for someone to wear a cross or head of Jesus around his neck when he plans to do something which we know would be opposite to the love of Christ. So these guys who terrorized their towns have no business hanging a rosary in the front window of their car. And when we plan on hurting another person, doing drugs, abusing alcohol, stealing, having sex with someone we don't even love, or using our mouths to communicate badly (cursing, swearing, saying things which are bigoted or ugly), we really have no place carrying or using symbols of Jesus or His Church. To do so mocks God and the beauty of the values Jesus died to teach us.

On the other extreme, we sometimes find good people who treat religious symbols with too much reverence. Religious articles point the way to God, but they are not God. I've seen people who revered statues of saints, but who thought little of walking past a tabernacle or ignoring other people. No symbol or statue or sign of the faith should supplant the real presence of Our Lord in the Eucharist or in His people. Religious symbols are a real treasure. They should never be used badly, either by a lack of reverence or too much reverence. They should, instead, be seen as helpmates on the journey of belief.

Questions for Reflection

- Does it bother you when rock stars make a mockery of religion by the misuse of religious symbols?

- Does it bother you when people pay too much attention to the symbols and not enough to the "human" temples of God?

Eating for Life

PAUL is 25 and a regular at the local gym. Graduated from a local college, he's still not sure about his direction in life. Like a lot of people, he's got some difficulties with commitment. He wants to be sure, in his choice of careers and in the person he marries, that he can live with his decisions. So while he assesses his life direction, he works out, eats right, plays some ball and keeps in good shape. Paul recently met a young woman who is equally concerned about staying healthy and fit. It fact, they met at the gym and have become a steady item. Indecisive about continued education, unsure about a career she can feel comfortable with, Donna's also discerning the road ahead.

I've known Paul for many years and so was intrigued and happy when he met this new girlfriend. He sounded very taken with her. And, in truth, he thought that if he could find it in his heart to commit to her, then perhaps the other decisions in his life would also make sense. I asked Paul what he liked the most about Donna. His first words, although understandable, were not a little disquieting. "She's got a fantastic body. She goes to the gym every day, she's in terrific shape. She's also got a face to match the body, a real knock-out," explained Paul. Only much later, with probing from me, did he also tell me that she was "sweet, kind, caring and thoughtful." In other words, Paul, like most of us, was first drawn to Donna's physical enticements. Personality and personal qualities came second or third. At least that's the message he sent.

Fast forward six months. Paul comes to see me with nervous concerns about Donna. He's even more in love with her now, but he's also worried for their future. Seems that Donna's got a problem with eating. Oh, she eats plenty. But none of it stays in her body very long. Because Donna, like scores of other women (and men to a lesser degree) suffers from a chronic eating disorder. Following most meals, she forces herself to bring the food back up. Donna binges and then purges. It's getting really serious. In fact, it may soon become life-threatening.

138 *Eating for Life*

Paul, when we met, talked as if this was strictly a problem Donna had. And, in fact, he still wanted to build their romantic relationship, talk of marriage surfacing from time to time. But I never witnessed Paul take any responsibility for Donna's "problem."

In fact, Paul is not entirely responsible for Donna's eating disorder. At least as important is Donna's problem with self-esteem. And is there any problem in the world which doesn't have some connection to our families of origin? Further inflaming her problems are a culture which tells us that we're only as valuable as the shape of our bodies. And Paul clearly passed this very message along to her. He told her, continuously, about how wonderful she looked. He constantly compared her beauty to the insufficiently beautiful women they'd see on the street. He communicated to her a sense of value based primarily on the cover of her body. Her waist, her chest, her bottom and her face were prized more than her heart, her mind, her soul and her sensitivities.

Donna told me that she began to be gripped with fear. If Paul thought so much of her body, would he still love and treasure her when her body changed or aged? And loving him as she does, she's become fixated on maintaining the image Paul loves, even at the cost of her health and well being.

We are, all of us, much more than what people see. And in matters of love, we should probably always begin the process of caring from the inside out. Love the shell and the love may well fade with time. Love the interior person, and you may have found a love that lasts forever.

Questions for Reflection

- How do you maintain a healthy attitude towards your body without going overboard?
- How can you help the Donnas you know?

Loving Yourself

MY friend Matt stopped by the church to say hello. Atop his head was standard gear for someone his age, a well-worn baseball hat. Since we were just inside the church, I took his baseball cap off and reminded him that we usually take our hats off in church as a sign of respect. Matt looked panicked telling me he had to keep it on because he had a bad case of "hathead." Hathead, for the uninitiated, means that your hair looks like a disaster area because you've had it crammed inside a hat all day. Now, Matt is one of the most confident-seeming people I know, so I was surprised to see his shock at the thought of going hatless.

My friend Danny works out at the local gym every other day. And whereas most folks working out wear shorts, sneakers and a tee-shirt, Danny is different, he wears sweatpants. I mean he's never without them. It can be boiling outside and even hotter at the gym, but Danny will not appear in public wearing shorts. I asked him about that one day. "Well," Danny confessed, "you've never seen my legs. I mean they are awful. I need to work on them really bad, Father Jim, they're practically stick figure legs! Now, if you knew Danny, this reaction would surprise you. On the outside, he's the epitome of confidence and self-possession.

Which reminds me of Meredith. She's a beautiful and talented young woman I've known through the parish for several years. She's a sensitive and delightful human being. She would be a catch for any guy lucky enough to land her. She has everything in the world going for her. One day, not long ago, Meredith came by to say hello. Well, she wasn't really there to say hello, she was there to talk about her boyfriend. Seems they'd been fighting a lot lately. And every time they would battle, Meredith would be reduced to tears. He'd tell her all the things that were wrong with her. He'd put her down in front of others. He'd tell her she wasn't thin enough, or pretty enough, or talented enough. He'd make her feel like she wasn't worth anything. When just the opposite is true. Meredith is a great lady. She truly has it all. So why, I wondered, is she staying with this clown who works so hard to make her feel awful? I asked Meredith that question. She told me that she used to think that she was okay. Then she started dating Kevin. Little by little he convinced her that she wasn't so special after all. She started to buy into his vision of her, and believe herself to be of very little value.

All of my friends: Matt, Danny and Meredith have some things in common. Each is a wonderful, warm, generous, attractive, good and delightful person. But each of them share other qualities of personality which are troubling. Each of them worries much too much about how they're perceived by others. And their personal sense of identity suffers because of a need to be a certain way in the eyes of others.

Living to please other people, especially our peers, is a waste of time and energy. We're not here on planet Earth to meet someone else's expectations; we're here to be happy and content with the person God made us to be. And the best way of evaluating our worth is interior. Knowing that we have a kind heart is infinitely more important than worrying about a case of hathead. Knowing that we're sensitive to the needs of other people is infinitely more vital than any bodily muscle group. Being a person of generosity and compassion is infinitely more important than meeting a boyfriend's or girlfriend's expectations of physical beauty. Because all the physical stuff lasts for just a while. The interior values, the interior beauty, is ours for a lifetime.

We live in a society which mistakenly pushes us to worry about how we look, how we dress, what we drive, how we smell, how we wear our hair, and how much money we make. The truth of our worth is simpler than all that. When we look in the mirror, do we find a person of truth, of kindness, of sensitivity of caring, of generosity and of value as a child of God? If we answer yes to that question, we really don't need to worry about too much else. Hair will fall out, legs may give out, beauty may pass, but our interior value is forever.

Questions for Reflection

- If you answered "yes" to Msgr. Jim's question in the last paragraph, you can pass Go and share your secret.
- If not, what do you think it takes to love yourself as a child of God?

On Divorce

MY friend June is one angry lady. Over thirty years ago she married a man she truly loved. It was her clear and unmistakable intention to spend the rest of her life with him. They had four terrific children, bought a nice home on Long Island, and seemed to be living out the American dream. Unfortunately, it was a dream which slipped into a full-throttled nightmare. Her husband grew apart from her. He invested his emotional and physical interests elsewhere. He treated her badly. Feeling unwanted and underappreciated also made her lose a sense of her own worth. She ate too much, slept too much and ultimately became disgusted with herself. Finally, her husband saw no reason not to go. One September he left June and moved in with his significantly younger girlfriend. Three months later they were expecting the first child of his new family. He divorced June and never looked back.

June's story is not unique. There are millions of people like her in our society—people who started their married lives with one set of expectations, only to see their dreams and hopes languish in the dustbin of disappointment and disillusionment. Recently, I found June even more angry and more defeated. She is still a practicing Catholic, and her faith is probably all that stood between her sanity and the worst kind of destructive depression. She takes what the Church says very seriously. So when the new Catechism was published, June read it with special interest. When she got to the chapter on divorce, her blood began to boil over. This is what the chapter says: "Divorce is immoral also because it introduces disorder into the family and into society. This disorder brings grave harm to the deserted spouse, to children traumatized by the separation of their parents and often torn between them, and because of its contagious effect which makes it truly a plague on society." (page 573, Section 2385). June was devastated. As she read it, her divorce made her "immoral" and responsible for the creation of a societal "plague." I've heard many other people read it with a similar interpretation. So let's see if they read it rightly. The Catholic Catechism is not calling anyone involved in a divorce immoral. It's saying, instead, that divorce as an institution is immoral. That it's always a tragedy to see the end of what was a loving union. In the black comedy "War of the Roses," lawyer Danny DeVito is asked, "Which one won the divorce, Mr. or Mrs. Rose?" DeVito replies, "No one won. Divorce isn't about winning. It's about degrees of losing." And in our country, where there's been a 750-percent increase in the number of divorces between the years 1901 and 1990, that losing has been acute.

No, the Church isn't condemning anyone who divorces. But the Church is saying that it has great empathy for the heartbreak which befalls everyone involved in divorce. We've got millions of formerly middle-income women with children who are living at or below the poverty line because of divorce. We've got millions of kids who almost never see the non-custodial parent because of divorce. And, perhaps most importantly, we've got a new generation of young people who are the children of divorce and who seriously doubt that any love can last forever. That cynicism about the possibility of enduring love is perhaps the most serious by-product of divorce. I wish that my friend June could find the peace she so richly deserves. But I think she's looking in the wrong place to direct her anger. The Church fully understands the suffering she has experienced through divorce. And the new Catechism is simply reminding us that there are truly no winners in the dissolution of a marriage.

Questions for Reflection

- Do you think there is a contagious effect of divorce?
- Do you feel there is a correlation between divorce and the failure of young couples to commit to marriage?

Movies That Uplift

WE live in fascinating times, especially when it comes to things of the media. By computer, or cable, or video, or DVD, we can see movies we may have missed when they first appeared on the scene. There are literally thousands of films produced in any given year, so it's hard to keep on top of it all. Some which may have slipped us by when they were first shown in theaters deserve to be caught in a later format.

One that's worth your time is called "Gattaca." Starring Ethan Hawke, Uma Thurman, Alan Arkin, Jude Law and Loren Dean, it's a futuristic tale about a civilization in which genetic manipulation will help us to produce a "super race" of people—people created without our human defects and imperfections. Thirty years ago, such a film would have been seen as an improbable fiction. Now, in light of genetic cloning, we know not only that it can happen, but certainly will. All of which makes this powerful cinema more arresting. It's written and directed by Andrew Niccol. You should watch it, discuss it, and let it motivate you to follow closely the frightening movement we're making toward a "brave new world" of so-called "human perfection." Thanks to the influence of my friend Father Andrzej, I've also learned the special advantage of watching movies on the DVD format. In many instances, these digitally mastered movies give you additional material you wouldn't have had a regular video tape. DVDs often include scenes that were cut from the original released film, but which add immeasurably to an understanding of the writer or director's intent. "Gattaca" includes such an addition in a section called the "coda." The text of this section reveals the mind of the creator. Listen to what he tells us:

"In a few short years, scientists will have completed the Human Genome Project, the mapping of all genes that make up a human being. We have now evolved to the point where we can direct our own evolution. Had we acquired that knowledge sooner, the following (imperfect) people may never have been born. Writer/Director Niccol then names but a few of the many less than perfect people we celebrate in history. People like President Abraham Lincoln (born with Marfan syndrome), or poet-author Emily Dickenson (who was afflicted with manic depression), or artist Vincent Van Gogh (who suffered from epilepsy), or scientist Albert Einstein (who was dyslexic), or President John F. Kennedy (who endured life-threatening Addison's disease), or actress Rita Hayworth (who had Alzheimer's disease), or singer Ray Charles (born with primary glaucoma), or Nobel Prize-winning scientist and author Stephen Hawkins (afflicted with amyotrophic lateral sclerosis) or Olympic Gold Medal champion Jackie Joyner-Kersee (who lived her life in the shadow of asthma). And then, to drive the point home that everyone is born with at least some imperfection, the director concludes with this startling statement: "Of course the other birth that may never have taken place is your own."

And while I'm talking about films we should not miss, let me suggest that you see "The Hurricane," starring Denzel Washington as boxer Rubin Carter. I believe it's the finest picture of the year. It fairly challenges us to examine what we mean by justice, and reminds us that racism is very much alive and poisonous (even as we fool ourselves into believing that color and ethnic differences don't matter anymore). Frankly, it's a much more truthful picture than the pro-abortion apologia "The Cider House Rules." That film attempts to lull us into a sugarcoated acceptance of abortion as a "humane" solution to life's difficulties. It will, no doubt, enjoy great success among the Hollywood set, but should be seen by us as the propaganda it is.

On another popular success, one from the realm of cable television, I need to offer yet another concern. Every award group is falling over itself to celebrate HBO's series called "The

Sopranos." And it is a well made series, populated by gifted actors. But it is, once again, a skewed view of Italian-American families. Less than a fraction of such families have anything even remotely to do with the Mafia. But by the entertainment industry's standards, to be Italo-American is almost equal to being part of organized crime. When we support this kind of programming, we lend help to those who will continue to stereotype Americans of Italian descent. Enough is enough. Let's see something truly positive about Italian-Americans for a change. The African-American community rightly protested their depiction in 1970s and 1980s films as criminals and drug addicts. Italian-Americans (and Catholics in general) should be equally vocal about this insidious effort to box us into a deeply artificial Hollywood construct. Movies and television can uplift and ennoble. Watch them wisely and critically.

Questions for Reflection

● What other movies and TV shows have you found morally and emotionally uplifting?

● Have you found that you can trust the critics?

Moving Beyond

OF all the kinds of appointments a priest makes in the course of a week, this one was the sort I've always hoped would never happen. A young man, in his mid-20s, called to say that he had a number of emotional issues to discuss which directly impacted on his faith. In fact, he told me that if he couldn't find some answers to questions which paralyzed him, he'd most likely be leaving the Church.

His issue was a big one. Seems that from the age of five until he was around 18, this young man had been the victim of sexual and emotional abuse. In itself, that's monumental. But it gets worse. The abuser was also a priest. Now, there are plenty of things which happen in Churches that we know aren't great, but nothing compares to the damage done to a young person at the hands of someone we hope he can trust and believe in. From a priest's point of view, these situations are especially painful because every time a story breaks about priestly abuse, all of us are tarred with this awful brush. Never mind that priestly violations of this kind are no greater or lesser than that of either married men or clergymen of other religions. When a Catholic priest abuses kids, it's big news of the worst sort. The young man (we'll call him Dan) was deeply hurt, badly depressed and looking for answers. More importantly, he was looking for a compassionate presence to listen, to understand, to bless and to heal. I was grateful, frankly that he was willing to even meet with a priest after the things he's been through.

The cost to this good man has been immense. He found it hard to trust anyone. He dated and was engaged to marry but feared that his lack of closure on this chapter of his life would sabotage any chance of a healthy married family life. He was terrified about his trust being betrayed again. He had guilt about his willingness to let the abuse continue as long as it did. Dan was filled with all the hurts, the needs and the pains which victims of abuse are left to suffer.

In trying to help him past the sorrows of his very wounded heart, I wanted to focus on three important truths.

First, no one who is victimized by another human being is responsible for the evil that other person commits. Dan had no reason to wonder about his cooperation. He was a child over-whelmed by an adult who should have known better. He needs to face the anger without asking confusing questions about his own culpability. Dan didn't choose the abuse. He is a victim.

Second, Dan's healing will move forward if he can separate the perpetrator from the institution for which that priest worked. All priests don't commit these heinous acts. A very small percentage of priests do. It is counterproductive and deeply unjust to paint every priest in the same corner as those who mistreat others. In the same way that I as an Italian-American shouldn't be held responsible for the crimes of that tiny portion of my people who make up the Mafia, so neither should priests bear the weight of responsibility for those few who tragically abuse children. The anger that Dan feels toward priests is something all of us can relate to. It's easier to lump people together, to generalize, than to see people one at a time. I am deeply saddened (and angry) over what that priest did to Dan. But all priests didn't do it.

Dan is also dealing with issues which transcend the priest-hood. He's wondering about a God who allows such evil to occur. After all, he figures, how "good" is a God who permits children to be abused? That's a question much bigger than his specific pain. It's a question any good person who experiences suffering deals with.

Truth is, God doesn't make any of the bad things happen. But loving us deeply as He does, He grants us a world in which we can freely choose to do good or evil. He hopes, sometimes against hope, that we'll choose rightly. In the end, I couldn't take away Dan's pain, I could only share the journey toward healing. And along that path to healing I hope that he (and anyone who's ever been wounded by someone in the Church) will recognize that:

—the Church is bigger and better than the wrong actions taken by any one of its people;

—while God doesn't make the bad happen, He understands why we might end up blaming Him, and He's big enough to carry the anger we feel, and

—none of us can move beyond our pain unless we find the capacity to forgive. In the end, our unwillingness to absolve those who wound us will only limit and paralyze us.

Dan's pain belongs to the Church, and by that I mean all of us. His healing and well-being are a prayer all of us should be offering.

Questions for Reflection

- What changes have you noticed in the way the Catholic Church handles clergy abuse today?
- How does the media influence your judgments about clergy abuse?

Selective Orthodoxy

ONE of the continuing criticisms of American Catholics, and especially those of a more liberal persuasion, is that they are "supermarket Catholics." The term implies a selective approach to obedience, a person who chooses to obey some Church teachings while ignoring others. On a typical trip down the aisles of a local supermarket, you can pick and choose what you like while ignoring the things you don't. Some suggest that Catholics approach Church teaching in much the same way.

Selective obedience is viewed in two very different ways. Some folks believe that examining an issue and choosing another direction implies a rejection of the Church. Others believe that the Church provides guidelines for living which we are obliged to consider and examine but that our intellect and the decisive role of individual conscience are also factors in the path we finally choose. I remember a day spent teaching couples who would be themselves instructors of marriage preparation on a parish level. After explaining each of the Church's teachings on sexual ethics, I also explained that they should teach only what the Church teaches, that as representatives of the Church, they had a moral obligation to be loyal to the Church's vision of truth. People who come to the Church to be taught aren't expecting, nor do they deserve, individual opinion alone. They can get that from you over a cup of coffee. In the setting of Church teaching, fidelity to what the Church actually teaches is probably the most honest way to behave. In fact, a few teaching couples chose to withdraw from leadership roles in their parish because of my suggestion. They could not, in good conscience, embrace all that the Church teaches. I thought their decision admirable but painful too. It would be easy but simplistic to suggest that a lack of faithfulness to Church teaching is territory only crossed by progressives. Frequently a disturbing drift off the reservation is occurring from conservative quarters as well. And these voices need the same call to fidelity. Let me highlight three examples.

Across America, Mother Angelica has an enormously powerful reach. Many good people, of a traditional stripe, view her with great admiration. And in many ways, she deserves their praise. From a humble beginning, Mother Angelica and her co-workers have fashioned a television empire of amazing influence. In many parts of the country, she is the only Catholic voice to be heard. She is a gifted woman. Not long ago, however, this self-described traditional Catholic went a statement too far. Giving her interpretation of a Pastoral Letter issued by Cardinal Roger Mahony of Los Angeles, Mother Angelica criticized the document. That would be difficult enough had it ended there. It didn't. She then went on to advise people living in the Archdiocese of Los Angeles to refrain from obedience to the author of the Pastoral Letter. In other words, she challenged the archbishop on national TV and seemed to suggest that disobedience was in order.

Now try to imagine what Mother Angelica herself would say were a liberal Church leader to suggest that another teaching, perhaps one closer to her conservative heart, should likewise be disobeyed. She would, rightly, consider that wholly unacceptable. And so was her criticism. Cardinal Roger Mahony, and every bishop of the Church, is appointed by the Holy Father. It is incongruous to suggest that we stand with the Pope while pillorying the leaders he appoints. Conservatives who "bash" bishops are guilty of precisely the same disloyalty they'd condemn in others. Disobedience is disobedience whether it comes from the left or from the right.

Recently, a priest decided that the bishops weren't doing enough to combat abortion. So he began a crusade to undermine and challenge the teaching authority of his bishop. In so doing, he directly disobeyed his religious community and the authority of the Holy Father who appointed the bishop. And the priest does all this in the name of "Catholic Truth." What poppycock! You can't have it both ways, Father. Condemning Catholics who practice in ways contrary to magisterial teaching while you disregard other teachings is inconsistency any way you slice it. A similar example occurred when the Holy See decided that young women could serve at the altar in a role once reserved to boys. I started getting mail from a number of "orthodox" Catholic groups encouraging opposition to the decision. Petitions and a letter-writing campaign were urged. But hold it! That permission for altar servers to include women came to us from the Vatican, and was without doubt run past the Pope. How can it be wrong for some Catholic groups to petition Rome for change in our rules, but all right when "orthodox" groups do it?

Accepting authority is easy for few. A thinking, nuanced person will always have difficulty with surrender to the will or teaching of an organization like the universal Church. At different stages of our lives, obedience comes more or less easily than it does at other times. But what is always necessary is consistency of evaluation. We cannot hold others to a standard we will not ourselves try to live. Liberals may well have a difficult time living in the Church. But if liberals are expected to embrace teachings without rebellion, then so must conservative or "orthodox" Catholics. That means an end to the Bishops Bashing, an end to the public criticisms of episcopal styles which might not be our own, and a willingness to accept and do the will of our spiritual shepherds. Obedience is not a discipline invented for some in the Church; it's a universal call for every one of us.

Question for Reflection

● How can you avoid selective obedience to Church rules and still maintain your freedom to make informed choices?

Of Piercing and Prejudice

IT'S not polite to stare. That's what we're told from the early years. But some folks make staring a real temptation. Take the young people populating record stores today, especially the ones behind the counter. They're practically crying out: "Please notice me!" The signal is sent through the phenomenon of body piercing. Metal studs inserted through the nose, the belly, the lips, the tongue, and just about anyplace you've got skin.

And so we play the game, trying to act like we're not staring, but finding it difficult not to drop a jaw. I mean, it's not like these folks are made more attractive by ripping up their heads or bodies. Quite the opposite. They look as though they must be in pain.

So, you may ask, what's the problem with body piercing? Well, it's not so much a problem as a symptom. It's an attempt to be different, and to be recognized as somehow unique. It's tied to a desire to rebel, to be seen as an outsider, a renegade, someone daringly different. I'm not sure it's a sin, but it sure doesn't show much respect for the beauty of God's creation. And it's certainly not going to please our parents, our teachers or most other adults in our life. So maybe that's the point. To stand apart, to establish a unique and separate identity. But isn't there an easier way? The body is a gift from God. It's meant to be treasured and respected. It's not a bulletin board for our latest posting of anger, rebellion or internal pain. If you're thinking about piercing your body, please think again. If you've already done it, take the damn things out. You'll look and feel a whole lot better about yourself. And maybe people will start to stare for the right reasons; not because you're boldly different, but because you reflect the beauty of God's incredible face.

And now a word about magazines. Teens buy them by the millions, they represent thirty percent of the magazine market and that translates into a billion dollar industry. So naturally, it's important to know what teenagers read. The folks at People magazine, the Big Guy on the magazine block want a share of that market. So they've started a new publication called Teen People. It looks just like their adult model, only a little trendy in layout. They ran an article recently telling America about teenagers choosing faith and religion. It was a terrible piece for Catholics. It either ignored our very existence or showed us to be the religion contemporary teens are leaving behind. It was, I'm afraid, typical of the ways many magazines present our Catholic Christian faith. It really bothered me, though, to see the same prejudices exercised against us in adult magazines being introduced into the teen market. It made me realize that we need to alert young readers to become protectively critical of what they read from an early age.

I wrote to the folks who run Teen People. Here's what I told them:

Dear Editor:

I was saddened but not surprised by your recent article "Choosing My Religion." Once again, media anti-Catholic bias reared its ugly and unacceptable head.

Catholics make up more than a quarter of the U.S. population. You'd never know that from the religions you suggest are being chosen by teens. More disturbingly, you highlight a Methodist and a Buddhist teen who have rejected their Catholicism. You ignore the fact that every year thousands of teens and young adults embrace the Catholic Church. Why not highlight the many who walk toward our wonderful faith instead of making it sound as if Catholicism is a religion to be denied?

You know things are out of hand when Teen People focuses more attention on an agnostic than on the millions of proudly Catholic teens in America.

A closing note of hope and encouragement: there is a youth magazine that proudly proclaims Catholic values: It's called

"You!" and it's excellent, fair-minded and wonderfully pro-Catholic. It's published on the West Coast. You can contact them for information by writing: "YOU!" 29963 Mulholland Hwy., Agoura Hill, California 91301. Or call them at 1 (818) 991-1813. Don't settle for magazines that mock us, trivialize us and put us down. Be proud. Be Catholic. And be informed.

Questions for Reflection

● What kind of identity are you hoping to establish?

● What are some other magazines or books that will help you be a proud and informed Catholic?

The Right Note

IN the classic old film "Angels With Dirty Faces," Jimmy Cagney plays a noted neighborhood gangster. As a tough criminal, he takes on a fame and a notoriety which impresses many of the teenagers who hail from his "poor" section of the city. His teen fans admire his toughness, his route to easy money and his ability to get away with his life of crime.

Finally, Jimmy goes a crime too far and gets nabbed by the police. His crime is murder, and he's sentenced to face the death penalty. Always a tough guy, even the threat of death doesn't upset or faze this career criminal. His blase response to the electric chair only widens the awe with which neighborhood kids emulate this guy. The popularity he enjoys troubles the local parish priest, played by the wonderful character actor Pat O'Brien. This local pastor realizes that if Cagney dies a hero to the teens of his neighborhood, others will embrace this loser lifestyle. In an honest man-to-man conversation, O'Brien explains to Cagney that if he really wants to be a help to the local kids, he must put aside his entrancing tough guy persona and die like a coward. This, in turn, will persuade the locals that being a criminal doesn't make you a superhero, it only affirms your loser status.

Cagney accepts the humiliating challenge. In transit to the electric chair, he fakes cowardice, being a mass of tears and pleadings. The neighborhood kids, reading all about it in the local newspapers, lose all regard for the thug they once put on a pedestal. In short, Cagney went the way he should. He left center-stage as the small and pathetic man he was, and in so doing, helped young people recognize what's truly valuable.

I recount "Angels With Dirty Faces" as a backdrop for the closing show of Seinfeld. Like this classic movie of the 1920's it ended just as it should. Jerry Seinfeld stayed true to the end, and that's very good.

Elaine, George, Kramer end Jerry should be role models for nobody. They're self-centered and entirely products of a me-first culture. They use people without regret. They live a highly promiscuous lifestyle. All hovering around 40, they've yet to embrace a permanent relationship. They love to make fun of others, and as the last episode demonstrated, they haven't got an ounce of the Good Samaritan in them. They're unsentimental and brutal in their put-downs of others. Their only loyalty is to themselves, and even their parents seem little more than bakdrops for their taunting humor.

And yet they made us laugh. They made us conspire with their jokes and enjoy their total self-absorption. Perhaps the constant focus on their own well-being made us feel we weren't so bad after all. I recall one of my friends, when he'd done something really self-centered saying, "well that's just my George Costanza side coming through." They made all of us look comparably pretty good.

All of which made the last show even more valuable. Because Jerry Seinfeld could easily have made us feel sentimental about this hapless crew. He could easily have given them some redeeming qualities for their final TV outing. He might easily have shown us some smidgen of their humanity, and that would've worked to convince us that maybe they weren't so bad after all. But he didn't.

Instead, with a remarkable integrity of purpose, he kept them constant to the end. He had us watch them watch a guy getting mugged. They not only fail to intervene on his behalf, but stand there mocking the poor soul getting robbed, utterly unconcerned for his welfare or his suffering. They then go through a trial wherein all their years of self-absorption are held up as evidence. The jury then convicts them, with the judge sentencing them to a "year removed from society." The show ends with our Seinfeld clan talking in jail, feeling or expressing no obvious regret over their lack of caring. Even after being put away for a lack of concern for humanity, they just don't get it. The Golden Rule means as little to them after the trial as it did before.

In putting them blithely behind bars Jerry Seinfeld seems to be agreeing with the judge: they really have very little purpose or meaning for the world. They're just as well removed from a society for which they care not at all.

Seinfeld made us laugh for nine years and for that we should be grateful. But he paid us the highest service in ending the show as he did.

He didn't change his characters, he didn't transform them, he didn't sentimentalize them: he just kept them who they are.

Like Cagney before him, Seinfeld left center-stage as he should, showing us that some folks just aren't worthy of being copied.

Questions for Reflection

- Name the people in the media you think are worthy of being copied?
- Why?

Additional Titles Published by Resurrection Press, a Catholic Book Publishing Imprint

A Rachel Rosary Larry Kupferman	$4.50
Blessings All Around Dolores Leckey	$8.95
Catholic Is Wonderful Mitch Finley	$4.95
Come, Celebrate Jesus! Francis X. Gaeta	$4.95
From Holy Hour to Happy Hour Francis X. Gaeta	$7.95
Healing through the Mass Robert DeGrandis, SSJ	$9.95
Our Grounds for Hope Fulton J. Sheen	$7.95
The Healing Rosary Mike D.	$5.95
Healing Your Grief Ruthann Williams, OP	$7.95
Heart Peace Adolfo Quezada	$9.95
Life, Love and Laughter Jim Vlaun	$7.95
Living Each Day by the Power of Faith Barbara Ryan	$8.95
The Joy of Being a Catechist Gloria Durka	$4.95
The Joy of Being a Eucharistic Minister Mitch Finley	$5.95
The Joy of Being a Lector Mitch Finley	$5.95
The Joy of Being an Usher Gretchen Hailer, RSHM	$5.95
Lights in the Darkness Ave Clark, O.P.	$8.95
Loving Yourself for God's Sake Adolfo Quezada	$5.95
Mother Teresa Eugene Palumbo, S.D.B.	$5.95
Practicing the Prayer of Presence van Kaam/Muto	$8.95
5-Minute Miracles Linda Schubert	$4.95
Season of New Beginnings Mitch Finley	$4.95
Season of Promises Mitch Finley	$4.95
Soup Pot Ethel Pochocki	$8.95
Stay with Us John Mullin, SJ	$3.95
Surprising Mary Mitch Finley	$7.95
Teaching as Eucharist Joanmarie Smith	$5.95
What He Did for Love Francis X. Gaeta	$5.95
You Are My Beloved Mitch Finley	$10.95
Your Sacred Story Robert Lauder	$6.95

For a free catalog call 1-800-892-6657